SIXTH EDITION

MOSAIC

Listening/Speaking

1

Jami Hanreddy

Elizabeth Whalley

Lawrence J. Zwier
Contributor, Focus on Testing

Mosaic 1 Listening/Speaking, Sixth Edition

Published by McGraw-Hill ESL/ELT, a business unit of The McGraw-Hill Companies, Inc.,
1221 Avenue of the Americas, New York, NY 10020. Copyright © 2014 by The McGraw-Hill
Companies, Inc. All rights reserved. Printed in the United States of America. Previous editions
© 2007, 2001, and 1995. No part of this publication may be reproduced or distributed in any
form or by any means, or stored in a database or retrieval system, without the prior written
consent of The McGraw-Hill Companies, Inc., including, but not limited to, in any network
or other electronic storage or transmission, or broadcast for distance learning.

Some ancillaries, including electronic and print components, may not be available to customers
outside the United States.

This book is printed on acid-free paper.

5 6 7 8 9 LKV 21 20 19

ISBN: 978-0-07-759520-3
MHID: 0-07-759520-3

Senior Vice President, Products & Markets: Kurt L. Strand
Vice President, General Manager, Products & Markets: Michael J. Ryan
Vice President, Content Production & Technology Services: Kimberly Meriwether David
Director of Development: Valerie Kelemen
Marketing Manager: Cambridge University Press
Lead Project Manager: Rick Hecker
Senior Buyer: Michael R. McCormick
Designer: Page2, LLC
Cover/Interior Designer: Page2, LLC
Senior Content Licensing Specialist: Keri Johnson
Manager, Digital Production: Janean A. Utley
Compositor: Page2, LLC
Printer: LSC Communications

Cover photo: LilKar/Shutterstock.com

All credits appearing on page iv or at the end of the book are considered to be an extension
of the copyright page.

The Internet addresses listed in the text were accurate at the time of publication. The
inclusion of a website does not indicate an endorsement by the authors or McGraw-Hill, and
McGraw-Hill does not guarantee the accuracy of the information presented at these sites.

www.mhhe.com

www.elt.mcgraw-hill.com

The McGraw·Hill Companies

A Special Thank You

The Interactions/Mosaic Sixth Edition team wishes to thank our extended team: teachers, students, administrators, and teacher trainers, all of whom contributed invaluably to the making of this edition.

Maiko Berger, **Ritsumeikan Asia Pacific University**, Oita, Japan • Aaron Martinson, **Sejong Cyber University**, Seoul, Korea • Aisha Osman, Egypt • Amy Stotts, **Chubu University**, Aichi, Japan • Charles Copeland, **Dankook University**, Yongin City, Korea • Christen Savage, **University of Houston**, Texas, USA • Daniel Fitzgerald, **Metropolitan Community College**, Kansas, USA • Deborah Bollinger, **Aoyama Gakuin University**, Tokyo, Japan • Duane Fitzhugh, **Northern Virginia Community College**, Virginia, USA • Gregory Strong, **Aoyama Gakuin University**, Tokyo, Japan • James Blackwell, **Ritsumeikan Asia Pacific University**, Oita, Japan • Janet Harclerode, **Santa Monica College**, California, USA • Jinyoung Hong, **Sogang University**, Seoul, Korea • Lakkana Chaisaklert, **Rajamangala University of Technology Krung Thep**, Bangkok, Thailand • Lee Wonhee, **Sogang University**, Seoul, Korea • Matthew Gross, **Konkuk University**, Seoul, Korea • Matthew Stivener, **Santa Monica College**, California, USA • Pawadee Srisang, **Burapha University**, Chantaburi, Thailand • Steven M. Rashba, **University of Bridgeport**, Connecticut, USA • Sudatip Prapunta, **Prince of Songkla University**, Trang, Thailand • Tony Carnerie, **University of California San Diego**, California, USA

Dedications

To my charming and indomitable students, who constantly inspired me to find ever fresher, more challenging, and "funnier" ways to meet their needs, met every challenge head on, and provided so many wondrous, hilarious, and inspiring stories. To Valerie Kelemen at the helm, who had the vision to go for a Sixth Edition, making our books quite likely the longest lived series in our niche, if not in all of creation, never lost her cool, and got going when it was toughest. To Anita Raducanu, editor extraordinaire, who, though still remaining "faceless" at the time of this writing, is the embodiment of grace, good humor, intelligent solutions, and "how to just get it done." To Gracie, Fred, and Emma, who curled up and waited patiently, until they decided I needed my exercise. And to Joe, top chef never to be chopped, whose love consummately provides the context for these efforts.

—Jami Hanreddy

Thanks and props to Jami who met all the deadlines and did most of the work, grueling and otherwise. To Mary Dunn whose light still shines. "Time is a gift in which to learn." And, of course, to the folks at the Plant.

—Elizabeth Whalley

Photo Credits

Table of Contents

A 21st-Century Course for the Modern Student

Interactions/Mosaic prepares students for university classes by fully integrating every aspect of student life. Based on 28 years of classroom-tested best practices, the new and revised content, fresh modern look, and new online component make this the perfect series for contemporary classrooms.

Proven Instruction that Ensures Academic Success

Modern Content:

From social networking to gender issues and from academic honesty to discussions of Skype, *Interactions/Mosaic* keeps students connected to learning by selecting topics that are interesting and relevant to modern students.

Digital Component:

The fully integrated online course offers a rich environment that expands students' learning and supports teachers' teaching with automatically graded practice, assessment, classroom presentation tools, online community, and more.

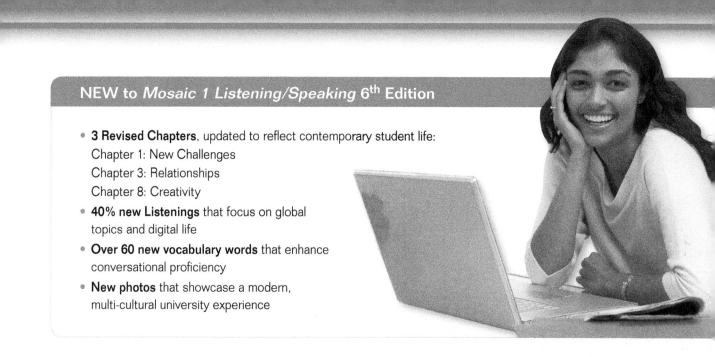

NEW to *Mosaic 1 Listening/Speaking* 6th Edition

- **3 Revised Chapters**, updated to reflect contemporary student life:
  Chapter 1: New Challenges
  Chapter 3: Relationships
  Chapter 8: Creativity
- **40% new Listenings** that focus on global topics and digital life
- **Over 60 new vocabulary words** that enhance conversational proficiency
- **New photos** that showcase a modern, multi-cultural university experience

Emphasis on Vocabulary:

Each chapter teaches vocabulary intensively and comprehensively. This focus on learning new words is informed by more than 28 years of classroom testing and provides students with the exact language they need to communicate confidently and fluently.

Practical Critical Thinking:

Students develop their ability to synthesize, analyze, and apply information from different sources in a variety of contexts: from comparing academic articles to negotiating informal conversations.

Highlights of *Mosaic 1 Listening/Speaking* 6th Edition

Part 1: Building Background Knowledge
Each chapter begins with facts and figures pertaining to an interesting contemporary topic. The activities that follow prepare students for developing important listening skills.

Did You Know?

- The human brain cannot possibly take in and remember all of the information presented during a typical lecture, yet this is the way most college students are taught, especially in their introductory courses.
- Because books were rare before the printing press, someone would often read a book aloud to others. In fact, the word *lecture* comes from the Latin word *to read.*
- From December 9–14, 2009, Errol Muzawazi of Zimbabwe gave a lecture on "Democracy" at Jagiellonian University in Krakow, Poland, that lasted 121 hours.
- According to Guinness World Record rules, Muzawazi could only take a short break every eight hours to eat, use the bathroom, and take a quick nap. His audience, however, not bound by the same rules, often slept while Errol talked to himself.

What Do You Think? In pairs, discuss the following questions.

1. Why do you think that most higher education courses after high school and even some high school courses are taught mainly through lecturing?
2. What types of skills would be important to have in order to get an "A" in a course that is taught entirely through lectures? Do you think that all intelligent people have these skills? Do you think that if you don't have these skills that you should simply give up and drop out of school? Why do you think so?
3. What do you think a lecturer should do if students are falling asleep during his or her lectures?
4. Is it the length or the content of a lecture that causes students to fall asleep, or perhaps something else? Why do you think so? Share a personal experience as an example, if possible.

Sharing Your Experience

Discussing Changes Think about the following questions and make a few brief notes to help you remember your thoughts. Then discuss your answers in small groups or as a class.

1. Many people think that a good teacher knows how to help you to dig deeply not only into a course topic, but also into yourself. Have you ever done any digging? How might digging to the core of Earth be like getting to know yourself?

▲ How is digging through Earth's layers like getting to know yourself?

2. Have you ever been in a situation where all of the expectations or rules were very different from what you were used to? This is a common experience when you visit another country, but it can happen even in your hometown. Try to recall an experience like this, or try to imagine yourself in a situation where all the rules are new. Include answers to the following:

- Where were you?

- What were the new expectations and rules?

- How did you figure them out?

- How long did it take you to get accustomed to the new expectations and rules and to feel competent or successful in this situation?

3. Have you ever taken a class in which the instructor did not lecture? If not, imagine you have participated in a course in which lecturing was not used.
- What took the place of lecturing? Did you feel comfortable with this method of teaching? Why or why not?

- How did you do on the tests for this course? Did you get a good grade? Did you understand the material better? Why or why not?

- Did you get to know the instructor and the other students better than in a lecture course, and do you think this was an important factor in your learning? Why or why not?

- Is memorizing all there is to learning? Or is there more to it? What might those things be?

Practical Critical Thinking
Key communication strategies that support language learning and encourage independent thinking are practiced.

Strategy

Predicting What the Instructor Will Say Next

Surprises can be nice in everyday life, but if they occur frequently in a lecture or other type of presentation, they may be difficult to understand. In order not to be surprised too often, it is useful to be ready for or anticipate what the instructor will say next. Here are two guidelines to help you make predictions.

1. Before you listen, think about (a) what you already know about the topic and also about (b) what you want to learn about the topic.
2. As you listen, predict what the speaker will say. When the speaker makes a statement:
   a. Predict what she or he will say next.
   b. Judge quickly whether you were right or wrong.
   c. If you were right, move on to your next prediction.
   d. If you were wrong, just put a question mark in your notes for clarification later and move on to the next prediction.

When you focus your listening in this way, you are less likely to be distracted by thoughts of things such as lunch, your soccer game, or the party you and your friend went to on Saturday night.

Before You Listen

1 Considering the Topic   Brainstorm answers to the following questions in small groups. Share one idea each time it is your turn and keep taking turns until your instructor says "stop." One person should write down your group's answers in the small circles of the graphic organizer so they can be shared later with the whole class.

Part 2: Listening to Make Predictions

Each chapter teaches crucial skills such as how to focus your listening and predict what a speaker will say.

Impactful exercises Engaging assignments draw students in, making learning more efficient and fun.

1. What comes to mind when you read the title of the presentation: "Don't Lecture Me: A New Paradigm for the University of the Future"?

2. What do you think the speaker will discuss?

3. What questions do you have on the topic?

Role-Plays With a partner, choose one of the previous nine situations to act out. You may either use a prediction that one of you wrote, or write a new one together.

1. Take 10 to 12 minutes to prepare your role-play.
2. Present your role-play to the class.
3. After each pair of students presents a role-play, share the predictions the class wrote about that situation.
   * Did anyone in the class predict what happened in the role-play?
   * Were your predictions similar, or were they different? If there were similarities, why do you think they happened?
   * If there were different predictions, do you think your individual perspectives or points of view about challenging situations account for the differences? Discuss why or why not.

PART 3 Offering and Requesting Clarification

 Strategy

Ways to Offer Clarification
We have all noticed that sometimes people don't seem to be following what we are saying. They might look confused, uncomfortable, nervous, or even tense as they try to understand. One way to make sure that people understand what we are saying is to offer clarification when it is needed. To do this, we can either repeat the information exactly or say it again in another way using different words.

Expressions to Offer Clarification

Appropriate for most situations:
* Are you following me?
* Are you with me?
* Did you get that?
* Do you understand so far?
* Does that make sense to you?
* Is that clear?
* OK so far?
* Right?

Appropriate only in informal situations:
* Did you catch that?
* Got it?

NOTE: Listeners are usually appreciative when you use these expressions to check whether or not they need clarification. But be careful with your tone of voice. You don't want to sound as if you were angry because they weren't listening.

Part 3: Offering and Requesting Clarification
Students learn to apply their listening and speaking skills to a variety of practical interactions such as offering clarification.

 Listening for Tone of Voice You will hear two conversations. In both conversations, the speakers use the same expression to try to offer clarification. Listen for the difference in tone between a helpful question and an angry, critical, or scolding one in each conversation. Then answer the questions.

Conversation 1
Ms. Torres is talking to a group of cruise ship employees.
1. Which of the expressions from the strategy box does Ms. Torres use?

2. What is her intention when she uses this expression?

Conversation 2
Mrs. Gobel is talking to her children.
Mrs. Gobel uses the same expression to offer clarification that Ms. Torres did in Conversation 1. What is Mrs. Gobel's intention when she uses this expression?

 Strategy

Understanding a Speaker's Style of Offering Clarification
When you listened to the presentation, "Don't Lecture Me: A New Paradigm for the University of the Future," did you notice that the speaker used several expressions for offering clarification? Using the same expressions repeatedly is part of a speaker's style. Being familiar with a speaker's style can help you understand the content of the presentation.

 Listening for Expressions that Offer Clarification Listen to the presentation "Don't Lecture Me" again. This time, notice which expressions the speaker uses to offer clarification. Each time the speaker uses an expression, put a check (✓) next to it.

_____ Are you following me?   _____ Is that clear?
_____ Are you with me?   _____ OK so far?
_____ Did you get that?   _____ Right?
_____ Do you understand so far?   _____ Did you catch that?
_____ Does that make sense to you?   _____ Got it?

Communication for the Modern Student A focus on real-life and academic communication prepares students for success in school and in life.

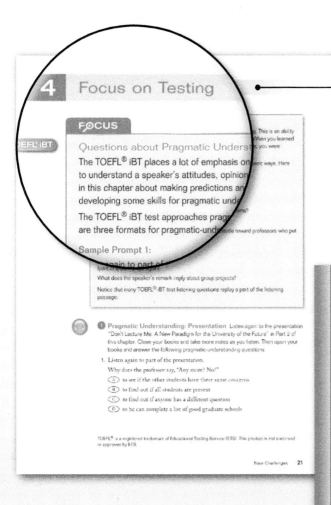

4 Focus on Testing

FOCUS

TOEFL® iBT

Questions about Pragmatic Understanding

The TOEFL® iBT places a lot of emphasis on ... to understand a speaker's attitudes, opinion... in this chapter about making predictions an... developing some skills for pragmatic und...

The TOEFL® iBT test approaches prag... are three formats for pragmatic-und...

Sample Prompt 1:

... gain to part of ...

What does the speaker's remark imply about group projects?

Notice that many TOEFL® iBT test listening questions replay a part of the listening passage.

🔊 ① **Pragmatic Understanding: Presentation** Listen again to the presentation "Don't Lecture Me: A New Paradigm for the University of the Future" in Part 2 of this chapter. Close your books and take more notes as you listen. Then open your books and answer the following pragmatic-understanding questions

1. Listen again to part of the presentation.
   Why does the professor say, "Any more? No?"
   Ⓐ to see if the other students have these same concerns
   Ⓑ to find out if all students are present
   Ⓒ to find out if anyone has a different question
   Ⓓ so he can complete a list of good graduate schools

TOEFL® is a registered trademark of Educational Testing Service (ETS). This product is not endorsed or approved by ETS.

New Challenges **21**

2. Listen again to part of the presentation.
   What is the professor's opinion about lectures?
   Ⓐ He thinks that professors and students should be allowed to use what they are used to.
   Ⓑ He thinks that they are not particularly effective.
   Ⓒ He thinks that they are a good way to teach and learn.
   Ⓓ He thinks that they create problems for both teachers and learners.

3. How do you think the professor would answer the student's question, "Can I get into a good graduate school from here?"
   Ⓐ Yes, but not easily.
   Ⓑ Yes, even though the process is mysterious.
   Ⓒ Perhaps. You can try.
   Ⓓ Yes. This program will prepare you well for any graduate program.

4. Listen again to part of the presentation.
   Why does the professor mention UC Santa Cruz and Alverno College?
   Ⓐ to show that the methods used at his university are well established
   Ⓑ to show that there are better programs than the one at his university
   Ⓒ to show that the programs at these schools are exactly the same
   Ⓓ to show that he is also very enlightened

5. Listen again to part of the presentation.
   The professor says, "Our program... is based on a set of student learning outcomes and objective rather than merely on faculty interests."
   What is the professor implying in this statement?
   Ⓐ that the students can choose their professors based on their interests
   Ⓑ that the professors are objectively concerned with student learning
   Ⓒ that the students will not be required to take a course on a particular topic merely because a professor is doing research on that topic
   Ⓓ that the professors have a lot of interests and will help students set goals for learning about those topics

Part 4: Focus on Testing Students learn how to prepare for typical college exams and international assessments.

Results for Students A carefully structured program presents and practices academic skills and strategies purposefully, leading to strong student results and more independent learners.

Scope and Sequence

Chapter	Features	Listening
	**Presentation:** Don't Lecture Me: A New Paradigm for the University of the Future **Learning Strategy:** Listening to Make Predictions **Language Function:** Offering and Requesting Clarification	Critical listening to make predictions about what a speaker will say next Listening for tone of voice that reveals intentions Listening for expressions that offer clarification
	**Lecture:** Penguin Partners at the Pole **Learning Strategy:** Distinguishing Main Ideas and Supporting Details **Language Function:** Asking for Confirmation of Understanding	Distinguishing main ideas and details in a lecture Listening for appropriate use of intonation with confirmation of understanding expressions
	**Lecture:** Mom Always Liked You Best **Learning Strategy:** Understanding Straw Man Arguments **Language Function:** Making Generalizations	Listening for straw man arguments Listening for data and details refuting straw man arguments Listening for expressions used for generalizations

Speaking	Critical Thinking	Vocabulary Building	Focus on Testing
Sharing personal perspectives on academic lecture styles	Analyzing past, present, and future lecturing styles	Determining meaning from context	Types of pragmatic-understanding questions
Brainstorming and sharing predictions about lecture content and real-world situations	Using a graphic organizer to categorize information	Categorizing to deepen understanding of concepts	
Using appropriate expressions to request and offer clarification in formal and informal situations	Using a graphic organizer to tap prior knowledge and enhance understanding	Understanding and using new vocabulary in discussions of lecturing styles	
	Predicting what an instructor will say next		
	Comparing and contrasting class predictions		
	Analyzing a lecturer's style		
Sharing personal observations of cooperation and competition	Speculating about penguin behavior	Matching vocabulary words to appropriate context	Pragmatic understanding of a speaker's attitudes, opinions, strategies, and goals
Collaborating to brainstorm plans for a scientific expedition	Using a graphic organizer to brainstorm plans for a scientific expedition	Understanding and using new vocabulary words in discussions of cooperation and competition	
Comparing outlining strategies with classmates	Predicting main ideas and supporting details		
Sharing predictions of main ideas and details of a lecture	Identifying main ideas and supporting details		
Discussing how to reach consensus on a controversial topic	Constructing a basic outline to sort out main ideas and details		
Presenting your views on a controversial topic	Using an outline to organize notes on a research topic		
Asking for confirmation of understanding during a lecture or informal presentation			
Making and challenging excuses in everyday situations			
Sharing perspectives on sibling and family relationships	Using a graphic organizer to compare and contrast sibling rank and relationships across cultures	Using definitions and contextual cues to place vocabulary words into sentences	Pragmatic understanding of a speaker's feelings and intentions
Comparing and contrasting cross-cultural differences in sibling rank and relationships	Distinguishing straw man arguments from main points	Writing about personal opinions and experiences to broaden understanding of new vocabulary concepts	
Critiquing the effectiveness of straw man arguments to change listeners' assumptions	Using an anticipatory guide to explore and test assumptions on a topic	Understanding and using new vocabulary words in discussions about sibling and family relationships	
Sharing assumptions about life experiences	Predicting straw man arguments	Paraphrasing and using synonyms to deepen understanding of vocabulary signaling generalizations	
Refuting others' assumptions	Critiquing the effectiveness of straw man arguments		
Interviewing someone in the community to check assumptions	Constructing effective arguments to refute assumptions		
Making generalizations	Doing research to check assumptions		
Paraphrasing generalizations	Using adverbs of time to make generalizations		

Scope and Sequence

Speaking	Critical Thinking	Vocabulary Building	Focus on Testing
Sharing prior knowledge about the heart and other body parts Comparing body parts to mechanical devices Discussing the effectiveness of analogies Brainstorming possible contexts for analogies Sharing analogies that have become common expressions in one's country Expressing personal opinions about health and fitness Role-playing characters involved in situations leading to debates about health issues	Using a graphic organizer to build background knowledge Understanding and using analogies Using a graphic organizer to chart analogies and what they mean Evaluating the effectiveness of an analogy Imagining possible contexts for analogies Distinguishing facts from personal opinions Choosing appropriate expressions to introduce opinions	Using definitions and contextual cues to place vocabulary words into sentences Understanding and using new vocabulary in discussions about the heart and health	**TOEFL iBT** Pragmatic understanding of opinions Expressing opinions on standardized tests
Sharing prior knowledge about space exploration and high-tech versus low-tech solutions Debating the pros and cons of the privatization of space travel Sharing Internet research on space exploration Collaborating to match labels to sequenced pictures of a space mission Saying numbers Describing the phases of a space mission and the use of the RMA Reporting a news event using passive voice	Analyzing the pros and cons of the privatization of space travel Utilizing specific strategies to get the most out of field trips Researching to build background knowledge Matching labels to sequenced pictures Identifying the parts and functions on a diagram Selecting relevant notes to give a summary Distinguishing uses of the active and passive voice	Using definitions and contextual cues to place vocabulary words into sentences Understanding and using new vocabulary in discussions about space exploration	**TOEFL iBT** Note-taking during listening passages
Sharing opinions about the importance of money Exploring relative values of modern conveniences versus preserving natural resources Sharing prior knowledge about and personal experiences with banks Brainstorming challenging questions about the World Bank Brainstorming ways to invest money Presenting ideas on ways to invest money Agreeing and disagreeing with things about the World Bank Supporting or challenging items in the news Simulation game: Planning for the prosperity of a nation	Evaluating the worth of a project Using a sunray graphic organizer to tap prior knowledge Identifying the pros and cons of banks Matching pro and con arguments Formulating challenging questions Evaluating whether answers are adequate or not Brainstorming, organizing, and presenting ideas to a group on the best ways to invest money Determining how to agree/disagree confidently, yet politely Supporting or challenging items in the news Speculating about how to make a country more prosperous	Using definitions and contextual clues to complete a crossword puzzle Understanding and using new vocabulary in discussions about money matters	**TOEFL iBT** Making inferences when listening to informal conversations and listening passages

Scope and Sequence

Chapter	Features	Listening

Speaking	Critical Thinking	Vocabulary Building	Focus on Testing
Sharing opinions about types of remarkable feats	Comparing/contrasting and ranking remarkable feats	Pooling knowledge with classmates to match words to definitions	Expressing preferences on standardized tests
Sharing stories about remarkable feats	Using a Venn diagram to show things groups have in common	Using new vocabulary to answer contextualized questions	
Collaborating to complete a Venn diagram of remarkable feats	Using time and sequence words as clues to chronological order		
Collaborating to put story parts into chronological order	Tuning in to the logic of chronological order		
Collaborating to complete a timeline of life events	Putting story parts into chronological order		
Telling a story in chronological order	Using a graphic organizer to sort events into general chronological time periods		
Reaching consensus on ways to express likes and dislikes, pleasure and displeasure in real world situations	Using a timeline to sort events into narrow chronological time periods		
Discussing likes and dislikes, pleasure and displeasure regarding goals and interests	Choosing appropriate ways to express likes and dislikes, pleasure and displeasure		
Sharing ideas about what motivates you at work, school, and play	Comparing kinds of creativity	Using definitions and contextual cues to place vocabulary words into sentences	Listening for signal words and other cues to take better notes during listening passages on standardized tests
Discussing different ways to become more creative	Identifying when and where you have been the most creative	Using new vocabulary in discussions about creativity	
Sharing puzzle and problem solutions that use your creativity	Solving a brainteaser puzzle		
Creatively using tone of voice and body language signals to communicate	Identifying the main points in a lecture on drive and creativity		
Completing and role-playing conversations containing divulged information	Identifying tone of voice and body language signals		
	Identifying whether "divulged" information is critical		
	Distinguishing and using appropriate ways to divulge information		

Speaking	Critical Thinking	Vocabulary Building	Focus on Testing
Speculating about behavior	Speculating about human behavior	Choosing definitions that fit words as they are used in particular contexts	
Discussing the benefits of volunteerism	Identifying and analyzing the reasons for digressions and returns to the main topic	Understanding and using new vocabulary in discussions about human behavior	Pragmatic understanding of transition phrases relating to digressions
Sharing preferences regarding time spent alone and time spent with others	Using a graphic organizer to chart predictions about, reasons for, and expressions introducing digressions		
Sharing prior knowledge about social behaviors	Analyzing groups dynamics		
Discussing the *whys* and *hows* of digressions in informal situations	Discerning subtle differences between genuine, rhetorical, and challenging tag questions		
Predicting and discussing digressions in a lecture	Using a graphic organizer to chart types and elements of tag questions		
Reporting to the class about digressions heard outside of class			
Discussing group dynamics			
Using tag questions to ask for information or confirmation, or to challenge			
Discussing if punishments fit their crimes	Paraphrasing what an instructor says about predetermination and free will	Pooling knowledge with classmates to match words to definitions	
Discussing whether "unfair" laws should be broken	Paraphrasing an instructor's wishes, hopes, and desires	Understanding and using new vocabulary in discussions about predetermination and free will	Answering idea-connection questions
Discussing harsh punishments as deterrents to crime	Distinguishing the subtle difference between hopes and wishes		Answering multiple-choice and table format questions
Sharing personal experiences with "wrongdoing"	Using graphic organizers such as tables and charts to organize information		
Sharing prior opinions about predetermination and free will			
Reading paraphrases aloud to classmates			
Paraphrasing issues/problems for group discussions			
Paraphrasing a speaker's wishes, hopes, and desires			
Sharing hopes and wishes			
Role-playing characters expressing hopes and wishes			

1 New Challenges

> "I never lecture, not because I am shy or a bad speaker, but simply because I detest the sort of people who go to lectures and don't want to meet them."

H.L. Mencken
American journalist and satirist

In this
CHAPTER

Presentation Don't Lecture Me: A New Paradigm for the University of the Future

Learning Strategy Listening to Make Predictions

Language Function Offering and Requesting Clarification

Connecting to the Topic

1. What is the most challenging thing you have ever done?

2. What is the most challenging thing about learning a new strategy or skill? What is the most rewarding?

3. What is the most challenging thing about working with strangers on a project?

Did You Know?

- The human brain cannot possibly take in and remember all of the information presented during a typical lecture, yet this is the way most college students are taught, especially in their introductory courses.
- Because books were rare before the printing press, someone would often read a book aloud to others. In fact, the word *lecture* comes from the Latin word *to read.*
- From December 9–14, 2009, Errol Muzawazi of Zimbabwe gave a lecture on "Democracy" at Jagiellonian University in Krakow, Poland, that lasted 121 hours.
- According to Guinness World Record rules, Muzawazi could only take a short break every eight hours to eat, use the bathroom, and take a quick nap. His audience, however, not bound by the same rules, often slept while Errol talked to himself.

1 **What Do You Think?**   In pairs, discuss the following questions.

1. Why do you think that most higher education courses after high school and even some high school courses are taught mainly through lecturing?

2. What types of skills would be important to have in order to get an "A" in a course that is taught entirely through lectures? Do you think that all intelligent people have these skills? Do you think that if you don't have these skills that you should simply give up and drop out of school? Why do you think so?

3. What do you think a lecturer should do if students are falling asleep during his or her lectures?

4. Is it the length or the content of a lecture that causes students to fall asleep, or perhaps something else? Why do you think so? Share a personal experience as an example, if possible.

Sharing Your Experience

2 **Discussing Changes**   Think about the following questions and make a few brief notes to help you remember your thoughts. Then discuss your answers in small groups or as a class.

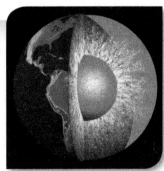

1. Many people think that a good teacher knows how to help you to dig deeply not only into a course topic, but also into yourself. Have you ever done any digging? How might digging to the core of Earth be like getting to know yourself?

▲ How is digging through Earth's layers like getting to know yourself?

_____

_____

2. Have you ever been in a situation where all of the expectations or rules were very different from what you were used to? This is a common experience when you visit another country, but it can happen even in your hometown. Try to recall an experience like this, or try to imagine yourself in a situation where all the rules are new. Include answers to the following:

- Where were you?

_____

_____

- What were the new expectations and rules?

_____

_____

- How did you figure them out?

_____

_____

- How long did it take you to get accustomed to the new expectations and rules and to feel competent or successful in this situation?

_____

_____

3. Have you ever taken a class in which the instructor did not lecture? If not, imagine you have participated in a course in which lecturing was not used.

- What took the place of lecturing? Did you feel comfortable with this method of teaching? Why or why not?

_____

_____

- How did you do on the tests for this course? Did you get a good grade? Did you understand the material better? Why or why not?

_____

_____

- Did you get to know the instructor and the other students better than in a lecture course, and do you think this was an important factor in your learning? Why or why not?

_____

_____

- Is memorizing all there is to learning? Or is there more to it? What might those things be?

_____

_____

3 **Determining Meaning from Context** The underlined words in the following sentences appear in the presentation. Write the letter of the correct definition beside each sentence.

Many people feel that lecturing is not ▶ always the best teaching method.

Sentences

1. _____ The head of the department decided that lecturing to students was not working and that a new paradigm for instruction had to be developed.

2. _____ The paradigm for instruction not only had to be new, but also efficacious.

3. _____ Many educators and students feel that lecturing is completely obsolete as a method for sharing knowledge.

4. _____ Lecturing presents us with a paradox. On the one hand, lecturing may be ineffectual and obsolete, but on the other hand, it is what we are used to.

5. _____ Nevertheless, some students remain successful in spite of boring lectures.

6. _____ The Educational Testing Service really began to shake things up when they totally changed the paradigm of the TOEFL®.

7. _____ When the ETS introduced the integrated skills paradigm for the TOEFL® iBT, it was applauded as an attempt to assess language the way it is used in the real world.

8. _____ Only those students that have a great capacity for both listening and memorization seem to do well in a "lecture only" class.

9. _____ It was a revelation to some students to hear that lectures were not effective and therefore would no longer be used as a method of instruction.

10. _____ Relaxing enough to be willing to play by entirely new rules in a new situation is something that can completely transform us.

Definitions

a. to disturb the usual pattern or way of doing something in a major or surprising way

b. to change the nature of something

c. a model, or exemplary method, system or arrangement of things

d. the ability to receive and hold something such as knowledge

e. having outlived its original usefulness or value; out of date

f. producing the desired effect; having the intended result; successful

g. something important or surprising that is disclosed or revealed for the first time

h. a statement/situation that presents opposing views as true at the same time

i. without the expected effect from something

j. made whole or complete by bringing together something's parts

4 Categorizing Fill in the following chart with a partner and share your answers with your classmates.

Things that are obsolete	Things that might transform you	Things that might shake things up	Things associated with paradigm shifts	Things that can be transformed
a typewriter	a scary experience	a politician that always tells the truth	new expressions come into the language	a caterpillar into a butterfly

Strategy

Predicting What the Instructor Will Say Next

Surprises can be nice in everyday life, but if they occur frequently in a lecture or other type of presentation, they may be difficult to understand. In order not to be surprised too often, it is useful to be ready for or anticipate what the instructor will say next. Here are two guidelines to help you make predictions.

1. Before you listen, think about (a) what you already know about the topic and also about (b) what you want to learn about the topic.
2. As you listen, predict what the speaker will say. When the speaker makes a statement:
   a. Predict what she or he will say next.
   b. Judge quickly whether you were right or wrong.
   c. If you were right, move on to your next prediction.
   d. If you were wrong, just put a question mark in your notes for clarification later and move on to the next prediction.

When you focus your listening in this way, you are less likely to be distracted by thoughts of things such as lunch, your soccer game, or the party you and your friend went to on Saturday night.

Before You Listen

1 **Considering the Topic** Brainstorm answers to the following questions in small groups. Share one idea each time it is your turn and keep taking turns until your instructor says "stop." One person should write down your group's answers in the small circles of the graphic organizer so they can be shared later with the whole class.

1. What comes to mind when you read the title of the presentation: "Don't Lecture Me: A New Paradigm for the University of the Future"?

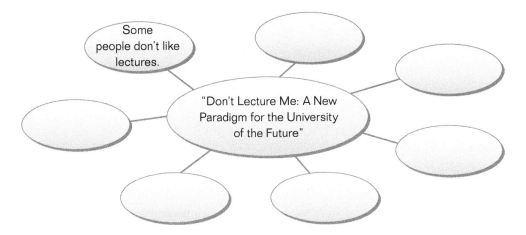

2. What do you think the speaker will discuss?

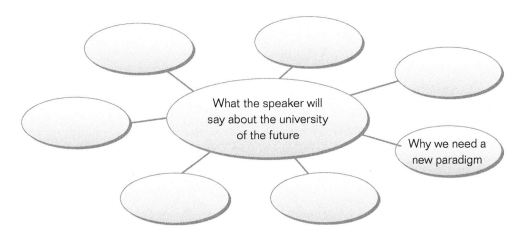

3. What questions do you have on the topic?

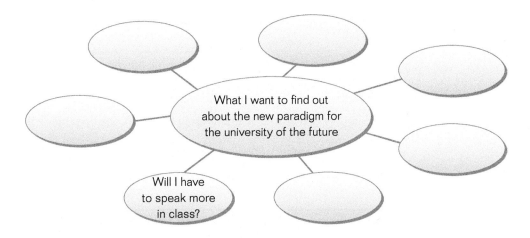

2 **Listening to Make Predictions** Listen to the presentation, one section at a time. After each section, try to predict what will happen next. Share your predictions with a partner. Then continue listening to see if your predictions were correct. If your prediction was not correct, write down what actually happened next.

Stop 1: *Just call out your questions.*

What questions do you think the students will ask?

_____

_____

Stop 2: *Then let's begin with the first question. Why not lecture?*

What do you think the presenter's answer will be to this question? Why?

_____

_____

Stop 3: *OK, so who decided that we needed a new paradigm for learning?*

What do you think the presenter's answer will be to this question?

_____

_____

Stop 4: *Their goal is to provide students with the tools they need to succeed in a world in which the information that they might memorize today could be totally obsolete in the future.*

What does this mean? What do you think will be discussed next?

_____

_____

Stop 5: *Our program… is totally based on a set of student learning outcomes and objectives rather than merely on faculty interests.*

What does this statement mean? What examples might be given?

_____

_____

Stop 6: *What if I can't figure out what's expected of me here?*

What advice or solutions do you think the presenter will offer?

_____

_____

3 **Comparing Predictions** Share your predictions from Activity 3 and what clues you used to make them with the whole class. You might want to listen to the lecture again and share your predictions at each of the stops about what is going to come next in the presentation. What did you learn from your classmates' predictions and their reasons for making them?

Talk It Over

4 **Making Predictions** Read the descriptions of characters and their situations. Then, write what you think will happen in each situation. Predict whether the characters will communicate well ("figure out the other's rules") or whether they will have a misunderstanding. Share your predictions in small groups.

1. **Characters**

   Character 1: Emma, 25 years old, never talks to strangers

   Character 2: Josh, also about 25, likes to be helpful and thinks people should be grateful for his help.

   Situation

   Josh and Emma are waiting to get on a bus. Josh sees that Emma's shoe is untied and that she might trip when she climbs the stairs of the bus.

   Your prediction:

   Example

   Josh tries to get Emma's attention, by clearing his throat, then calling out
   "Miss, Miss!" several times, but she doesn't listen. She trips as she is
   boarding the bus and falls back into his arms.

   Example

   Josh taps Emma on the shoulder, but she doesn't turn around. He taps again
   and this time she turns and looks for help from the other people standing
   there. She looks frightened, so he doesn't talk to her and just points to her
   shoe. She smiles gratefully.

   Example

   Josh gets in front of Emma in the line, then turns and tries to talk to her.
   She assumes that he is either rude or trying to pick her up and she ignores
   him. He shrugs and thinks, "OK, then. I tried." and gets on the bus. She
   trips, falls forward, and skins her knee on the steps.

2. Characters

Character 1: Jason, a 16-year-old boy who wants to be a rock musician. He is having trouble in history class. He keeps falling asleep

Character 2: Mr. Falco, Jason's history teacher

Situation

Jason wants to be a musician, but he must graduate from high school first. The problem is that he is failing history. The teacher thinks it is because he keeps falling asleep in class, but Jason thinks there is another reason. They meet to discuss the situation.

Your prediction:

_____

_____

_____

_____

3. Characters

Character 1: A shy young man, 26 years old, who prefers dealing with only familiar situations

Character 2: A confident young woman, 25 years old, who loves trying new things

Situation

The couple met a year and a half ago. She would like to get married and travel around the world for a year before settling down. He would like to get married, continue working in his father's factory, and buy the house next door to his parents for them to settle down in right away.

▲ Will she get her wish?

Your prediction:

_____

_____

_____

_____

4. **Characters**

    Character 1: Said, a doctoral student and teaching assistant in chemical engineering, has been brought up in a very hierarchical culture where there are special ways to address parents and teachers.

    Character 2: Jeremiah, an undergraduate in the course for which Said is a T.A., has been brought up in an environment where parents and teachers are your "friends."

Situation

Jeremiah spots Said in the cafeteria. He would like to have lunch with him so he calls out, "Hey, man! Said! Over here!"

Your prediction:

_____

_____

_____

_____

5. **Characters**

    Character 1: Rani, a 20-year-old student who is buying food for her family

    Character 2: Larry, a grocery store clerk who is also a student and a friend of Rani's

Situation

Rani is trying to use the machine in the self-checkout line, but she is having trouble. Every time she tries to scan an item and put it into her shopping bag, a loud alarm sounds. Larry notices that Rani is getting more than just a little frustrated and that she has begun to complain about the machine to all of the people in the line behind her.

Your prediction:

_____

_____

_____

_____

▲ It is not always the older people who are afraid of change.

6. Characters

Character 1: Zheng Quan, a father living in Hong Kong

Character 2: Zheng Yao, his 15-year-old son

Situation

Zheng Quan's son Zheng Yao has been offered a scholarship to study ballet in Boston, but he doesn't really want to leave Hong Kong, his high school, and all his friends. Zheng Quan doesn't understand why his son isn't excited about this amazing opportunity. They are discussing this problem at breakfast.

Your prediction:

_____

_____

_____

_____

7. Characters

Character 1: Simon, an "A" student who has just gotten an "F" grade for the first time on a midterm exam

Character 2: Professor Lee Hung, who is a visiting professor from Korea.

Situation

Simon thinks the test is unfair because it is not the kind of test he is used to. He goes to the professor's office to ask to take a different test with questions that he understands.

Your prediction:

_____

_____

_____

_____

8. **Characters**

Character 1: Mitch, the father of 6-week-old triplets

Character 2: Peggy, the mother of the triplets

Situation

Mitch and Peggy are sitting on their front porch, drinking tea and discussing what they will do when Peggy's two-month baby leave is over in a couple of weeks and she must go back to work. She suggests that perhaps Mitch might take a two-month leave from work as well.

Your prediction:

_____

_____

_____

_____

9. **Characters**

Character 1: Marti, a young nurse who has just moved to the United States

Character 2: Raul, her supervisor at work

Situation

Marti does not understand the accent nor the handwriting of a doctor that she must work with daily. This situation could be very dangerous for the patients, but Marti doesn't know what to do. She goes to her supervisor for advice.

Your prediction:

_____

_____

_____

_____

5 **Role-Plays** With a partner, choose one of the previous nine situations to act out. You may either use a prediction that one of you wrote, or write a new one together.

1. Take 10 to 12 minutes to prepare your role-play.

2. Present your role-play to the class.

3. After each pair of students presents a role-play, share the predictions the class wrote about that situation.

- Did anyone in the class predict what happened in the role-play?
- Were your predictions similar, or were they different? If there were similarities, why do you think they happened?
- If there were different predictions, do you think your individual perspectives or points of view about challenging situations account for the differences? Discuss why or why not.

PART 3

Offering and Requesting Clarification

Strategy

Ways to Offer Clarification
We have all noticed that sometimes people don't seem to be following what we are saying. They might look confused, uncomfortable, nervous, or even tense as they try to understand. One way to make sure that people understand what we are saying is to offer clarification when it is needed. To do this, we can either repeat the information exactly or say it again in another way using different words.

Expressions to Offer Clarification

Appropriate for most situations:
- Are you following me?
- Are you with me?
- Did you get that?
- Do you understand so far?
- Does that make sense to you?
- Is that clear?
- OK so far?
- Right?

Appropriate only in informal situations:
- Did you catch that?
- Got it?

NOTE: Listeners are usually appreciative when you use these expressions to check whether or not they need clarification. But be careful with your tone of voice. You don't want to sound as if you were angry because they weren't listening.

1 **Listening for Tone of Voice** You will hear two conversations. In both conversations, the speakers use the same expression to try to offer clarification. Listen for the difference in tone between a helpful question and an angry, critical, or scolding one in each conversation. Then answer the questions.

Conversation 1

Ms. Torres is talking to a group of cruise ship employees.

1. Which of the expressions from the strategy box does Ms. Torres use?

_____

2. What is her intention when she uses this expression?

_____

Conversation 2

Mrs. Gobel is talking to her children.

Mrs. Gobel uses the same expression to offer clarification that Ms. Torres did in Conversation 1. What is Mrs. Gobel's intention when she uses this expression?

_____

Strategy

Understanding a Speaker's Style of Offering Clarification

When you listened to the presentation, "Don't Lecture Me: A New Paradigm for the University of the Future," did you notice that the speaker used several expressions for offering clarification? Using the same expressions repeatedly is part of a speaker's style. Being familiar with a speaker's style can help you understand the content of the presentation.

2 **Listening for Expressions that Offer Clarification** Listen to the presentation "Don't Lecture Me" again. This time, notice which expressions the speaker uses to offer clarification. Each time the speaker uses an expression, put a check (✓) next to it.

_____ Are you following me?   _____ Is that clear?

_____ Are you with me?   _____ OK so far?

_____ Did you get that?   _____ Right?

_____ Do you understand so far?   _____ Did you catch that?

_____ Does that make sense to you?   _____ Got it?

3 Sharing Your Data Discuss these questions with your classmates.

1. Which expressions seem to be the speaker's favorite ones?
2. Which ones doesn't he use?
3. Did you need clarification when the speaker offered it?
4. Were there times when you needed clarification and the speaker did not offer it?

Strategy

Ways to Request Clarification

When you are the speaker and you notice that the listener isn't following you, it isn't easy to stop and offer clarification. When you are the listener, however, you cannot be certain that the speaker will know when you need clarification. Therefore, when you don't understand what someone is saying, don't wait for offers of clarification. Request information when you need it, even if you have to politely interrupt the speaker.

▲ Politely interrupt when you need clarification.

Polite Expressions for Interrupting to Request Clarification

One of these:	Followed by one of these:
Could/Can/May I interrupt?	Would you mind repeating that?
Excuse me.	Could/Would you repeat that, please?
Pardon me.	Could/Would you say that again, please?
I beg your pardon.	I didn't get the last part (word, etc.).
I'm sorry.	What was that again?

Informal Expressions for Requesting Clarification

Huh? (very informal)	What?
I didn't get the last part (word, etc.).	What did you say?
I didn't catch that.	You lost me.

4 Requesting Clarification During a Lecture or Presentation Listen to the presentation again.

- If you are listening to the presentation during class, raise your hand when you do not understand something. Your instructor will stop the recording and you may request clarification from the instructor or from a classmate. Practice using a variety of new expressions. Be sure to use new expressions and not only the ones you are already familiar with. Be ready to help your classmates when they request clarification.

- If you are listening to the presentation by yourself, stop the recording whenever you do not understand something and practice requesting clarification. Practice using a variety of expressions. Put a check (✓) next to each expression as you use it.

Talk It Over

5 Brain Teasers Work with a partner to solve the following challenging problems. Some of them are riddles (questions with unexpected answers) and others are "brain teasers" (problems that make your brain work very hard). When you have done all the problems with your partner, compare your answers with those of your classmates. (The answers are on page 215.)

Follow these steps and be sure to take turns and practice being both the listener and the speaker.

1. **Speaker:** Read the problem silently, and then read the problem aloud to your partner as quickly as you can. Do not pause at all.

   Listener: Keep your book closed. Do not read along with your partner. If you do not understand something, ask for clarification. Use one of the expressions for requesting clarification.

2. **Speaker:** Read the problem again. This time, slow down a little and frequently use expressions to check if your partner needs clarification.

   Listener: Tell your partner if you still need clarification.

3. **Speaker:** Slow down even more if necessary.

   Listener: Try to solve the problem.

Problems

1. How much is 10 times 9 times 0 times 5 times 2 times 10 times 7 times 8 times 4 times 1?

2. You're standing at three light switches at the bottom of stairs to the attic. Each one corresponds to one of three lights in the attic, but you cannot see the lights from where you stand. You can turn the switches on and off and leave them in any position. How can you identify which switch corresponds to which light bulb if you are only allowed one trip upstairs?

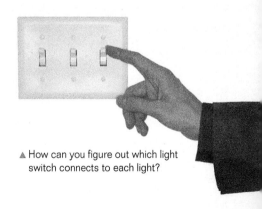

▲ How can you figure out which light switch connects to each light?

3. I am a word of five letters. People use me to make something to eat. If you remove my first letter I become a form of energy. If you remove my first two letters, I become something you must do to live. If you scramble my last three letters, I become something delicious to drink. What am I?

4. You have a three gallon jug and a five gallon jug. You need to measure out exactly seven gallons of water. How do you do it?

5. If a rooster laid 13 eggs and the farmer took eight of them and then another rooster laid 12 eggs and four of them were rotten, how many of the eggs were left?

6. A man is trapped in a room with only two possible exits: two doors. Through the first door, there is a room constructed from magnifying glass. The blazing sun instantly fries anyone or anything that enters.

▲ After you do the math, how many eggs are left?

Through the second door, there is a fire breathing dragon. How does the man escape?

7. You and a good friend go out and have lunch together, and the bill is $25. You and your friend each pay $15 in cash, which your server gives to the cashier. The cashier hands back $5 to the server. The server keeps $3 as a tip and hands back $1 to each of you. So, you and your friend paid $14 each for the meal, for a total of $28. The server has $3, and that makes $31. Where did the extra dollar come from?

▲ Did the server bring back the correct change?

FOCUS

Questions about Pragmatic Understanding

The TOEFL® iBT places a lot of emphasis on pragmatic understanding. This is an ability to understand a speaker's attitudes, opinions, strategies, and goals. When you learned in this chapter about making predictions and listening for tone of voice, you were developing some skills for pragmatic understanding.

The TOEFL® iBT test approaches pragmatic understanding in a few basic ways. Here are three formats for pragmatic-understanding questions.

Sample Prompt 1:

Listen again to part of the lecture:

[part of lecture plays again]

Why does the speaker mention several other university programs?

Sample Prompt 2:

Which of the following best describes the speaker's attitude toward professors who put students to sleep with their lectures?

Sample Prompt 3:

Listen again to part of the lecture.

[part of lecture plays again]

What does the speaker's remark imply about group projects?

Notice that many TOEFL® iBT test listening questions replay a part of the listening passage.

1 **Pragmatic Understanding: Presentation** Listen again to the presentation "Don't Lecture Me: A New Paradigm for the University of the Future" in Part 2 of this chapter. Close your books and take more notes as you listen. Then open your books and answer the following pragmatic-understanding questions.

1. Listen again to part of the presentation.

   Why does the professor say, "Any more? No?"

   Ⓐ to see if the other students have these same concerns

   Ⓑ to find out if all students are present

   Ⓒ to find out if anyone has a different question

   Ⓓ so he can complete a list of good graduate schools

2. Listen again to part of the presentation.

   What is the professor's opinion about lectures?

   (A) He thinks that professors and students should be allowed to use what they are used to.

   (B) He thinks that they are not particularly effective.

   (C) He thinks that they are a good way to teach and learn.

   (D) He thinks that they create problems for both teachers and learners.

3. How do you think the professor would answer the student's question, "Can I get into a good graduate school from here?"

   (A) Yes, but not easily.

   (B) Yes, even though the process is mysterious.

   (C) Perhaps. You can try.

   (D) Yes. This program will prepare you well for any graduate program.

4. Listen again to part of the presentation.

   Why does the professor mention UC Santa Cruz and Alverno College?

   (A) to show that the methods used at his university are well established

   (B) to show that there are better programs than the one at his university

   (C) to show that the programs at these schools are exactly the same

   (D) to show that he is also very enlightened

5. Listen again to part of the presentation.

   The professor says, "Our program... is based on a set of student learning outcomes and objective rather than merely on faculty interests."

   What is the professor implying in this statement?

   (A) that the students can choose their professors based on their interests

   (B) that the professors are objectively concerned with student learning

   (C) that the students will not be required to take a course on a particular topic merely because a professor is doing research on that topic

   (D) that the professors have a lot of interests and will help students set goals for learning about those topics

Self-Assessment Log

Check (✓) the words in this chapter you have acquired and can use in your daily life.

Nouns	Verbs	Adjectives	Expression
▦ capacity	▦ shake up	▦ efficacious	▦ in spite of
▦ paradigm	▦ transform	▦ integrated	
▦ paradox		▦ obsolete	
▦ revelation			

Check (✓) your level of accomplishment for the skills introduced in this chapter. How comfortable do you feel using these skills?

	Very comfortable	Somewhat comfortable	Not at all comfortable
Listening to make predictions	☐	☐	☐
Understanding expressions such as *Are you with me?* and *OK so far?* when used to offer clarification	☐	☐	☐
Using expressions such as *Are you with me?* and *OK so far?* to offer clarification	☐	☐	☐
Using expressions such as *Would you mind repeating that?* and *What was that again?* to request clarification	☐	☐	☐

Think about the topics and activities in this chapter and complete the statements.

In this chapter, I learned something new about _____

_____

I especially liked (topic or activity) _____

_____

I would like to know more about _____

_____

_____

2 Cooperation and Competition

> "Do not have the delusion that your advancement is accomplished by crushing others."
>
> Marcus Tullius Cicero
> Roman philosopher

In this
CHAPTER

Lecture Penguin Partners at the Pole

Learning Strategy Distinguishing Main Ideas and
Supporting Details

Language Function Asking for Confirmation of
Understanding

Connecting to the Topic

1. What are the penguins in the photo doing? How does it help
   them to survive?

2. How is this behavior similar to some human behaviors you have
   observed?

3. In what situations might penguins stop cooperating and become
   competitive?

Did You Know?

- Antarctica, the continent that surrounds the South Pole, is the coldest region of the world. It is entirely covered by an icecap and the warmest it ever gets is 32 degrees Fahrenheit (0 degrees Celsius). Most of the animals in this region live in the surrounding ocean, because only birds and a few insects and animals can survive exposed to the wind in this cold land. In fact, several species of insects live only in the fur or feathers of animals and birds to avoid freezing to death.

▲ Paradise Bay, Antarctica

- Emperor penguins need to be social and cooperative to survive the hardship of winter in Antarctica. During the coldest and windiest winter nights, they stand shoulder to shoulder in a tight pack called a *turtle*. After a while, when the penguins in the middle of the pack get warm, they exchange positions with those on the outside.

- There are 17 species of penguins in Antarctica but none in the Arctic. This is probably because there are no land predators in Antarctica such as the bears, wolves, and foxes that are found in the Arctic. There are, however, the skuas, predatory birds that will steal eggs and even baby penguins if adult penguins do not cooperate to protect their young.

1 **What Do You Think?** Discuss the following questions in pairs.

1. In general, do you think the basic nature of animals, birds, and insects tends to be more cooperative or more competitive? Give examples of cooperation and competition that you've observed.

2. What about people? Do you think humans are instinctively more cooperative or competitive? Give examples of human cooperation and competition that you've observed among your own family members and friends.

Sharing Your Experience

2 **A Scientific Collaboration** Working in small groups, imagine that you are zoologists about to begin a study of cooperative behavior of penguins with two or three other scientists. To prepare for your field study, which will include trips to Antarctica, fill in the following chart with the other "zoologists" on your team.

- Work cooperatively with your team to reach consensus—decisions you all agree on—then write your ideas on the chart.
- Copy your chart onto poster paper.
- When you are finished hang your chart on the wall. Compare your team's chart with the charts of the other "teams of scientists."

▲ Penguins are one of the few species that can survive in Antarctica.

Preparation for Expedition to Antarctica							
Facts about penguins that we want to learn	Who we will take with us and why	Supplies we will need to take and why	How we will travel (by bus, train, plane, boat, sled?)	Where we will have to stop on the way	How much time we will stay at each location	Dangers we will face	When, where, and how we will observe penguins
			by bus	the airport			

3 **Vocabulary in Context** The following words will be used in the lecture. Complete the sentences with the appropriate words. Then compare your answers with a partner.

awkward	Celsius	ecosystem	ferocious
battle	desolate	Fahrenheit	migratory
beachfront	disposition	to fast	to teem
catastrophic			

1. My friends say that since I like _____ areas, empty places with no people, I should move to Antarctica.

2. The _____ property along the coast of Antarctica would probably not be the best place to have a summer home, unless you were a penguin, of course.

3. _____ floods that destroy plant and animal life in a large area could change the biological patterns of the world.

4. Penguins are _____ birds that travel great distances every year, even though they cannot fly.

5. The word _____ refers to a network of interdependent relationships among organisms, including both plants and animals.

6. A temperature of 32 degrees _____ is 0 degrees _____.

7. Some birds eat a lot to store fat in preparation for when they need _____ during times when they cannot get food.

8. Once the dark winter is over and the baby penguins break out of their shells, the activity level increases and the penguin colonies or "towns" begin _____ with life.

9. The penguin's usual _____ is playful and curious, but if you attack one of their babies, watch out! Then they can become angry and ready to fight a _____ with you.

10. A _____ attack by a sea leopard might kill a penguin.

11. On land, penguins seem very _____, but in the water, they move very gracefully.

Distinguishing Main Ideas and Supporting Details

- Most lectures have a single overall main idea. It is the one idea that you can state briefly when a classmate asks you, "What was the lecture about?" In most cases, there are several other main ideas in addition to the overall one. These main ideas are the messages that the lecturer wants you to remember.
- Lecturers present examples and details to support the main ideas. Facts and illustrations may come before or after the main idea that they support. It is easier to pick out main ideas and understand the lecture as a whole if you can identify the order in which the speaker is presenting the main ideas and details.

Strategy

Identifying Main Ideas and Supporting Details

If you can identify whether the lecturer is using the deductive or inductive method of presenting ideas it will be easier to sort out the main ideas from the details. The deductive method starts with a main idea, followed by several examples or details that support it. The inductive method starts with the details and builds up to the main ideas.

Deductive	Inductive
Main Idea I	Examples or Details I
Examples or Details I	Main Idea I
Main Idea 2	Examples or Details 2
Examples or Details 2	Main Idea 2

Lecturers sometimes mix these two ways of presenting information, which can be confusing. If an instructor does this, it is a good idea to rewrite your notes as soon as possible after class. Rewriting helps you identify the main ideas, distinguish them from supporting details, and clarify anything that is confusing to you.

A good way to keep track of which examples and supporting details go with which main ideas is to use an outline. Basic outlines can help you briefly and clearly organize the information from a lecture (or a reading). Outlines are also very useful tools for reviewing before tests.

Strategy

Making a Basic Outline of Main Ideas and Details

Below is an example of a typical outline. The main points in an outline are always represented by roman numerals (I, II, III, etc.), and major examples and details are represented by capital letters (A, B, C, etc.). Subpoints, or more minor details, are represented by Arabic numerals (1, 2, 3, etc.).

I. _____

   A. _____

   B. _____

II. _____

   A. _____

   B. _____

III. _____

   A. _____

      1. _____

      2. _____

   B. _____

Before You Listen

1 What's Happening? Discuss the following photos in small groups. What do you think these penguins are doing? Why?

2 Predicting Main Ideas and Supporting Information Before you listen to the lecture "Penguin Partners at the Pole," study the following partial outline of information about penguin mating and nesting habits. With a partner, discuss what kind of information (main idea or major or minor supporting example or detail) is missing from the outline and then what the information might be.

I. Mating habits of penguins

    A. Need for order leads penguins to build nests in rows

    B. Order often interrupted by small wars between penguins

        1. _____

        2. _____

    C. _____

    D. Losers move to edge of nesting ground

        1. Steal unguarded eggs

        2. _____

Listen

 3 Listening for Main Ideas and Supporting Information Listen to the first half of the lecture, up to the description of what the "losers" do at the edge of the nesting ground. Pay special attention to the part about mating habits. Then with a partner, listen to the first half of the lecture again and together, fill in the information missing from the outline in Activity 2.

 4 Constructing an Outline Listen to the rest of the lecture. Pay special attention to the parts about nesting, feeding, and taking care of chicks. Then listen to the second half of the lecture again, taking notes to fill in the outline on page 32. Compare and combine your notes with a partner to improve your outline.

▲ A happy penguin family

II. Penguin nesting

_____

_____

_____

_____

_____

_____

III. Penguin feeding
   A. Long marches

_____

_____

_____

_____

_____

   B. Danger of predators

_____

_____

_____

_____

_____

IV. Care of orphaned chicks

_____

_____

_____

_____

_____

_____

5 **Comparing Outlines** Share your outlines with the whole class. Transfer the outline that you and your partner created to large pieces of paper so that you can easily share them with the rest of your classmates. Discuss similarities and differences in the ways the outlines are constructed and in the information that each pair considered important.

Talk It Over

6 **Sharing Prior Knowledge of a Topic** In this section, you will have an opportunity to present your views on a topic. To expand on what you already know about the topic, first discuss it in small groups using the following questions to guide your discussion.

> **Topic:** In the ecosystem discussed in the lecture, Adelie penguins have one main enemy—the sea leopard. But many animals are hunted by people, who can use the dangerous power of technology as a weapon. For example, the use of technology to kill whales has caused a worldwide controversy.

1. Why are whales hunted?
2. What parts of the whale are used and for what purposes?
3. What methods are used to hunt whales?
4. What is Greenpeace? What does it do?
5. Should whales and other endangered species be protected?
6. Some people want to cooperate to find a solution to this problem; others are more competitive and do not care to consider another view. How could people reach a consensus on this issue?

▲ Due to whaling, the practice of hunting whales, there are only an estimated 20,000 humpback whales left in the world.

7 Choosing a Position In your group, come to a consensus on the following issues concerning whales. If your group prefers, you may choose another endangered animal to research and discuss.

1. Are the methods used to hunt whales (or another animal) acceptable or not? Why?

2. Should governments control the way in which whales (or another animal) are hunted? The way in which all creatures are hunted? Why and how?

3. Which groups are concerned with this issue? Why?

4. What would be the best way to reach a consensus on this issue?

8 Researching a Topic of Study For homework, do an Internet search to find information to further your own ideas about hunting whales or another endangered species. Use the following keywords: *Greenpeace, whale hunting, whaling, endangered species.* If your group has chosen a different endangered animal, simply change your search keywords to include this animal along with the term *endangered species.*

▲ A protester tries to change consumer habits.

9 Making an Outline to Discuss Your Views Make a brief outline of your views on hunting whales or another endangered species and why you feel this way. Your position on each issue is a main idea and should be listed after a Roman numeral. Under the Roman numerals, list your supporting information after capital letters and Arabic numerals. Remember: It is your clearly stated supporting information that often will persuade people of your point of view.

10 Presenting Your Views to a Group Using only your outline as notes, present your views to your classmates and explain your reasons for your point of view.

Strategy

Using Appropriate Intonation and Expressions When Asking for Confirmation of Understanding

Even when you have heard and understood every word, it is still sometimes difficult to know exactly what a speaker means. In this case, you should ask the speaker for confirmation of your understanding. A good way to do this is to state what you heard in your own words and then ask if you understood correctly. To confirm that you have understood without insulting the speaker, you must ask your questions carefully. Your intonation can make you sound either cooperative or competitive, polite or insulting. When you are sincere and are asking a genuine question, your tone will sound cooperative and polite to the listener. However, if you use a sarcastic tone, you will sound competitive or even insulting.

Expressions for Asking for Confirmation of Understanding

Use one of these expressions:	Followed by one of these:
I'm not sure I understand.	Do you mean that...?
Professor, am I/is this right?	Are you saying...?
I'm not sure I'm getting this.	Is it...?
I don't know exactly what you mean.	Do you mean to say/imply that...?

With friends or family, you can confirm something less formally by omitting the first sentence and using only one of the second sentences listed. Or you may simply ask, "You mean...?"

1 **Listening for Appropriate Expressions and Intonation** Listen to the following conversations and answer the questions. Make sure to consider the speakers' tone of voice. Then discuss them with your classmates.

Conversation 1

At the side of the road, a lost driver is asking a police officer for directions.

Did the lost driver ask for confirmation appropriately? _____ Why or why not?

_____

_____

Conversation 2

Here is a conversation between a professor and a student.

Did the student respond appropriately? _____ Why or why not?

_____

Conversation 3

Here is a similar conversation between the same professor and student.

How do you feel about the student's confirmation strategy?

_____

_____

Conversation 4

In this conversation, a student is talking to an administrative assistant about

the preregistration procedure.

How would you react if you were this administrative assistant?

_____

_____

Conversation 5

Here is another conversation between the administrative assistant and

the student.

What is the main difference between Conversations 4 and 5?

_____

_____

 2 Asking for Confirmation During a Lecture Listen to the lecture again. This time, your instructor will stop the lecture after each of the sentences below. With a partner, practice using the expressions on page 35 to ask for confirmation of your understanding of each of the sentences.

Stop 1: It seems strange that this hard land could be the spring and summer home of a migratory bird—the penguin.

> **Example** Are you saying that they live there only half the year?

Stop 2: It is here, to this little bit of beachfront, that the penguin comes to mate and raise babies. It would be a little cold for us at this beach, though.

Stop 3: Because of this need for order, penguins build nests in perfect rows and the nesting area looks very much like the streets of a city.

Stop 4: They steal unguarded eggs, disturb nests, and play jokes on the happy couples.

Stop 5: ... and, of course, there are the skuas—the predatory birds that come down from the sky to eat the eggs and even baby penguins.

Stop 6: In the water, they play various water sports that they've invented while they fill themselves up with krill and other small sea animals.

Stop 7: Oh, yes. Penguins share everything. And they love to visit with neighbors, explore nearby ice floes or islands, and even climb mountains, following the leader in long lines up the mountainside.

Stop 8: When it is given, they begin their swim back to their winter home on another part of the continent.

▲ Parental protection is crucial for these penguin twins.

③ Asking for Confirmation of Understanding During a Presentation
Work in small cooperative groups for this activity. Imagine that you and your group members have jobs developing new technology. You have just invented a new product that you think will make everyone's life easier. Decide as a group what that product is, what it does, and how it works. For example:

- A TV with a mouse that allows you to click on a speaker's mouth and get an instant translation. This device also interprets bird and animal languages, such as penguin chirps and whale songs.
- An electromagnetic device that can be attached to your tongue to help you speak animal languages (or pronounce English correctly; or never say an angry, sarcastic thing again).
- A brain wave adjuster that will reduce competition and aggression in all species, including humans.

Next, take turns with the other groups presenting your unusual products. Imagine that you are trying to convince your boss that making and selling this product will be profitable. Make sure that everyone in your group participates and is responsible for a part of the presentation.

- When you are listening, interrupt politely in order to clarify the descriptions the other groups are giving.
- When your group is speaking, be ready to answer any and all questions about your invention.

Strategy

Asking for Confirmation to Challenge Excuses

Have you ever given an excuse that was not the truth for something you forgot or did not want to do? Did the other person believe you? Or did the other person question what you said, trying to confirm their understanding?

Consider these examples:

Conversation 1

Student: I'm sorry. I don't have my homework because my partner didn't cooperate and do his share of the work.

Teacher: I'm not sure I understand. Do you mean to say that you didn't attempt to do your work because he didn't do his work?

Conversation 2

Woman: No, I can't go to the movies with you because I have to help my friend with her homework.

Man: I don't get it. That's what you said last night. You mean you help her every night?

Notice how the teacher challenges the student in the first example and the man challenges the woman in the second example. They don't actually say the other person is lying, but it is clear that they suspect this. However, even by challenging a speaker, you may not get the truth. By asking for confirmation in a gentle tone of voice, however, you may be able to politely get the truth.

Talk It Over

4 **Making and Challenging Excuses** In pairs, practice the following pattern. Then role-play your conversation for the class.

Pattern

You:	Make an excuse for something you don't want to do.
Your partner:	Ask for confirmation, questioning the truth of the excuse.
You:	Make another excuse.
Your partner:	Ask for confirmation again, questioning the truth of the excuse.

Example

Student:	I'm sorry. I don't have my homework because my dog ate it.
Teacher:	I'm not sure I understand. Do you mean to say that your dog likes to eat paper?
Student:	Well, yes he does, actually. He has some sort of vitamin deficiency, I think.

Teacher: I'm not following this. Are you telling me that paper has nutritional value?

Student: You see, when he was a puppy he was taken away from his mother too soon and...

Teacher: Wait, am I right? Do you mean to tell me that you don't have your homework because your dog had an unhappy childhood?

▲ "Are you saying that the dog ate your homework?"

FOCUS

Developing Your Pragmatic-Understanding Skills

Pragmatic understanding of a speaker's attitudes, opinions, strategies, and goals is important in informal situations as well as on formal tests such as the TOEFL® iBT. When you learned in this chapter about ways people ask for confirmation of understanding and how intonation can reveal attitudes, you were developing your pragmatic-understanding skills.

1 Pragmatic Understanding: Brief Conversations Listen to the brief conversations and answer the questions that follow.

Conversation 1

What is the speaker implying?

A Frank is not strong enough.

B Frank is taking too many courses for his first semester.

C First-year students usually take this many courses.

D Frank has a lot of different interests.

Conversation 2

How is this student feeling and why?

A She is feeling sick because she is tired and hungry.

B She is happy because she doesn't have to use the meal plan on weekends.

C She is unhappy because she thinks the meal plan is too expensive for what she is getting.

D She is very angry because she can't buy food on Sundays.

2 **Pragmatic Understanding: Lecture** Listen again to the lecture "Penguin Partners at the Pole" from Part 2 of this chapter. Close your books and take more notes as you listen. Then open your books and answer the following questions.

1. Listen again to part of the lecture.

   Why does the professor say, "Did I say bird?"

   Ⓐ because he thinks he made a mistake in the pronunciation of the word

   Ⓑ because he wants to make sure that the students understand this word

   Ⓒ because he is calling attention to the fact that the penguin is a very unusual bird

   Ⓓ because penguins are not really birds

2. Listen again to part of the lecture.

   What is the professor's opinion about the penguins' choice of a home site?

   Ⓐ He thinks that they will not survive because it is too cold.

   Ⓑ He thinks it is amusing that they nest on "beachfront property" that might be very attractive to people if only it wasn't so cold.

   Ⓒ He thinks that mating and raising babies on an ice dome is dangerous.

   Ⓓ He thinks that the domestic life of penguins is strange.

3. Listen again to part of the lecture.

   What is the student implying by saying, "I think we have a few of those hooligan types in this class"?

   Ⓐ Some students are causing trouble in the class.

   Ⓑ Some students have been stealing things.

   Ⓒ Some students are losers and will never find a mate.

   Ⓓ Some students that don't have mates like to tease the ones that do.

4. Listen again to part of the lecture.

   Why does the professor mention the movie *Jaws*?

   Ⓐ to take a break from the main topic

   Ⓑ to explain how the sea leopard kills penguins

   Ⓒ to explain the similarities between sharks and sea leopards

   Ⓓ to help them picture the sea leopard by comparing it to something else they may already know about

5. Listen again to part of the lecture.

   Why does the student say, "Hear that, you guys?" (Choose two answers.)

   Ⓐ to point out that male penguins help their mates more with the children than some men do

   Ⓑ to point out that some of the students are not listening and may be missing something important

   Ⓒ to make sure that the men in the class have understood the point of this exchange between the student and the professor

   Ⓓ to make sure that everyone can hear the professor

Self-Assessment Log

Check (✓) the words in this chapter you have acquired and can use in your daily life.

Nouns	Verbs	Adjectives	
▩ battle	▩ fast	▩ awkward	▩ desolate
▩ disposition	▩ teem	▩ beachfront	▩ Fahrenheit
▩ ecosystem		▩ catastrophic	▩ ferocious
		▩ Celsius	▩ migratory

Check (✓) your level of accomplishment for the skills introduced in this chapter. How comfortable do you feel using these skills?

	Very comfortable	Somewhat comfortable	Not at all comfortable
Listening for main ideas and supporting information to construct an outline	☐	☐	☐
Using expressions such as *I'm not sure I'm getting this* and *Do you mean to imply...* to ask for confirmation of understanding	☐	☐	☐

Think about the topics and activities in this chapter and complete the statements.

In this chapter, I learned something new about _____

_____

_____

I especially liked (topic or activity) _____

_____

_____

I would like to know more about _____

_____

_____

3 Relationships

"If you want to know how your girl will treat you after marriage, just listen to her talking to her little brother."

Sam Levenson, American humorist

"I made a snowman and my brother knocked it down and I knocked my brother down and then we had tea."

Dylan Thomas, Welsh poet

"Siblings are the people we practice on, the people who teach us about fairness and cooperation and kindness and caring—quite often the hard way."

Pamela Dugdale, writer and sibling, as quoted in *Time*

 Connecting to the Topic

1 What are the relationships of the people in the photo?

2 One child is not happy. Whose fault might that be?

3 Who has the major responsibility to ensure happiness in the family?

Did You Know?

- A crested-penguin mother will kick the smaller of her two eggs out of the nest in order to take better care of what she thinks is the healthier chick in the bigger egg. Similarly, at the dawn of history, human parents may have favored the biggest, healthiest children since those kids would be more successful at surviving and thus ensuring that more of the family's genes would go into the next generation.

- First-born children are often the parents' favorite and this favoritism has a big payoff. A 2007 Norwegian study of more than 240,000 brothers revealed that first-borns had a three point higher IQ score over younger children in the family, partly as a result of getting the exclusive attention of parents in their first months or years. It was also found that, on average, the IQs of second children rose if the first-born died.

- First-borns are often described as conscientious, conservative, disciplined, power hungry, fearful of losing face, and generally more anxious than their siblings. More presidents and Nobel laureates are first-borns than other siblings.

- Last-borns, or the babies in the family, are usually the most creative, flexible, sensitive, willing to take risks, and extroverted in the family.

1 **What Do You Think?**

In pairs, discuss the following questions.

1. Are you happy with your birth order? If yes, why? If not, which birth order would you have preferred and why?

2. Besides a higher IQ, what might be some other advantages of being the first-born? What might be some of the disadvantages?

3. Were you a favorite child of one or both of your parents? Or perhaps the favorite of a grandparent or aunt or uncle? Whether you answer yes or no, what were both the advantages and disadvantages of being in your position of esteem or value in the family?

▲ First-borns are often their parents' favorite.

2 Considering Cross-Cultural Differences in Sibling Rank and Relationships Think about the questions in the chart below.

- Make some brief notes about your ideas.
- Share your ideas in small groups. Use your own family members, friends, or people you've heard about as examples in your discussion.

▲ How do these brothers feel about each other?

	In your native country and/or family...	In the U.S. or Canada...
Who is typically the favorite child? Oldest? Youngest? Most talented? Smartest? Prettiest? Male? Female?		
What are the feelings of the other siblings toward a favorite child?		
What do children do to compete for their parents' attention? Try to be the best at something? Cheat? Lie? Fight? What else?		
Does the competition and fighting between siblings ever get physical? Is this acceptable?		

3 **Vocabulary in Context** The following words are some key terms used in the lecture. Complete the sentences with the correct forms of the vocabulary words. Then compare your answers with your classmates.

Words	Definitions
arrogance	*pridefulness or self-importance that is often offensive*
entitlement	*a feeling of deserving or having a right to whatever you desire*
family dynamics	*inner workings of the family; interactions of family members*
household	*people living under one roof; generally a family living together*
longevity	*long life*
miss the mark	*to guess wrong*
siblings	*brothers and sisters*
spouse	*a husband or wife*
statistics	*a collection of numerical data*
syndrome	*a group of symptoms occurring together and characterizing a specific disease*

1. Pax has two brother and three sisters, so he has five _____.

2. The _____ of a human is most often greater than that of a dog.

3. The Census Bureau of the United States keeps track of the number of family members living in each _____.

4. These _____ are used by the government to make decisions about programs for the people in an area.

5. Your parents telling you how beautiful and smart you are all the time might lead to _____ instead of the quiet confidence they were hoping for.

6. Similarly, if you are your parents' favorite and they always give you everything you want, it may lead to a sense of _____ so that you expect the rest of the world to do the same.

7. Jack and Meg's child was born with a _____ that included a heart condition, difficulty learning to read, and very short fingers, but they loved her for her sweet disposition, and she was still their favorite.

8. When people get married, we typically say they are now husband and wife, not husband and _____.

9. When everyone in the family is getting along well, we say that the _____ are great.

10. If you guess that most people in the United States have at least six siblings, you will definitely _____.

4 Using Vocabulary Make some brief notes to answer each question. Then share your answers in small groups.

Vocabulary Word	Notes
1. Do you have any siblings? If yes, what are their ages? If not, would you like to have some? Why or why not?	
2. How many people live in your household now? Who are they?	
3. Describe the dynamics in your household. What would you say is the most important quality of these dynamics?	
4. What is it that can be annoying about arrogance? About a sense of entitlement?	
5. Do you think that statistics always lead to correct assumptions? Why or why not?	

PART **2** Understanding Straw Man Arguments

Strategy

Distinguishing Straw Man Arguments from Main Points

If you were to fight with a man made of straw, you would probably win. Thus, a "straw man" argument is an argument that can be defeated easily. Many straw man arguments are based on assumptions, or beliefs, people have that are not true.

Many professors feel that part of their job is to help students examine their assumptions. Therefore, instructors will often use straw man arguments in their lectures. For example, they will make a statement from one point of view (the straw man argument), and later they will demonstrate why this point of view is not accurate (defeat the straw man argument).

Because professors use straw man arguments so frequently, it is very important for students to distinguish between the straw man argument and the main point the professor is trying to make opposing the straw man argument. One way to get a head start on this is to try to anticipate straw man arguments by brainstorming your own assumptions about the topic and then "testing" these assumptions as you listen.

Strategy

Using an Anticipatory Guide to Test Assumptions and Predict Straw Man Arguments

The lecturer is going to speak about sibling dynamics in the United States. The chart in the following activity is an "anticipatory guide." In the two empty columns you will write down your assumptions about the questions in the first column. Organizing your thoughts in this way will help you to test your assumptions about this topic and to focus on the speaker's main points as you listen to the lecture.

1 Considering Your Assumptions Write brief answers to the following questions about siblings and their parents. Then discuss your answers in small groups.

	In your community	In the United States
What is the family relationship that is most likely to have the greatest longevity?		
What assumptions do you think people make about families in which adult siblings are highly competitive?		
What assumptions do you think people make about families in which adult siblings always get along?		

◄ What assumptions might you make about these two sisters?

2 **Predicting Straw Man Arguments** Based on the assumptions you've made about siblings and families, what straw man arguments do you think the lecturer might discuss in a lecture titled "Mom Always Liked You Best"? Share your ideas in small groups and then share your group's list with the whole class.

Straw Man Arguments the Lecturer Might Discuss

1.

2.

3.

4.

5.

3 **Listening for Straw Man Arguments** Listen to the lecture once all the way through just to get the gist, or the general ideas. Don't worry if you cannot understand every word. Then listen again.

- Listen particularly for the straw man arguments and why they are untrue.
- As you listen, jot down any questions you have so that you can note the answers after listening a second time.

4 **Listening for Data and Details Refuting Straw Man Arguments** Listen to the lecture again. This time listen for some specific numbers or data and other details. Mark your answers to Questions 1–3. Then continue listening and fill in the information about some of the straw man arguments.

1. What percentage of people in the United States have at least one sibling?
   - (A) 50
   - (B) 60
   - (C) 70
   - (D) 80

2. Why are sibling relationships often the longest relationships?
   - (A) because they know each other from "beginning to end"
   - (B) because they typically live longer than dogs
   - (C) because parents most often die before their children
   - (D) all of the above

3. What percentage of siblings in the U.S. have similar memories about their childhoods?
   - (A) 75%
   - (B) 25%
   - (C) data not provided by the professor

4. Straw man argument 1: _By and large, siblings who grow up under the same_
   roof will have similar impressions or memories about family interactions.
   _____
   _____

   Information the professor uses to defeat argument 1: _____
   _____
   _____
   _____

5. Straw man argument 2: _____

_____

_____

_____

Information the professor uses to defeat argument 2: _____

_____

_____

_____

6. Straw man argument 3: _____

_____

_____

_____

Information the professor uses to defeat argument 3: _____

_____

_____

_____

7. Straw man argument 4: _____

_____

_____

_____

Information the professor uses to defeat argument 4: _____

_____

_____

_____

5 **Examining Ways to Defeat Straw Man Arguments** In small groups, discuss the information the professor used to defeat the straw man arguments. Consider the following questions in your discussions and fill in the chart below.

1. Was any of this information surprising to you?

2. Was the professor successful in changing some of your assumptions? Why or why not?

Information that was surprising to me...	Assumptions I changed my mind about...

Talk It Over

6 **Sharing Ideas Based on Assumptions** Work in small groups. Each person in the group should choose one of the following situations. It's all right if more than one person chooses the same situation. Also, it may be more interesting or fun if you choose a situation that you have not experienced yet.

▲ What assumptions might you make about the children and adults in this family?

- An elderly person who has not seen his or her siblings in 50 years
- An only child of a single parent
- A parent of four teenagers who are always fighting
- A person whose siblings were always very supportive
- A person whose siblings were always very cruel
- A child who is the youngest of eight children
- A young adult who is the oldest of eight children
- A teenager who is the middle child of five children

Take two minutes to think about the situation you have chosen. What is daily life like for the person in this situation? If you have not had the experience you have chosen, make guesses about the person's daily life. Then take five minutes to list as many assumptions as you can. Then share your ideas with the rest of your group. Did anyone in your group disagree with your ideas? Could anyone convince you that your assumptions were not accurate? How?

My guesses or assumptions	Classmates' arguments that made me change my mind

Strategy

Doing Research to Check Assumptions
When making guesses or assumptions about something, it is best to find a source (a book, an article, a person) that can confirm that the assumptions are true and not false.

7 Checking Your Assumptions If possible, interview someone in the community who is currently in the situation you chose for the previous activity. If you can't find someone in that situation, select someone in a different situation. Ask about this person's daily life. Remember to ask about some of the guesses or assumptions that you and your group members have made.

Share the results of your interview with the class. Did any of your guesses turn out to be false assumptions that could be used as straw man arguments? Discuss which ones were false, and why.

Strategy

Generalizing with Adverbs of Time

When making statements about things that can be counted, try to be accurate.

Example
Of the 240,000 siblings in the study, 90% felt that their parents definitely loved one of their children more than the others.

However, sometimes you don't know the exact numbers. You cannot be accurate, but you do have some general ideas or opinions. In these cases, describe what you think happens *most* of the time by making a generalization. Generalizations often contain adverbs of time. Listed below are adverbs of time and other expressions used to make generalizations.

Adverbs of Time and Other Expressions Used for Generalizations

When things happen frequently, use:	When things happen infrequently, use:
by and large	hardly ever
for the most part	rarely
generally	seldom
generally speaking	
in general	
in most cases	
more often than not	
normally	
often	
overall	
typically	

1 **Paraphrasing Generalizations** Work in small groups. Discuss the meaning of each sentence. Then using another expression from the box above, write a sentence that means the same thing.

Example

By and large, parents lie to their children when the children come crying to them, accusing them of playing favorites, saddened by the unfairness of it all.

Typically, parents lie to their children about playing favorites.

1. Typically, parents will deny loving one child more than another.

2. We generally don't think of the elderly giggling and gossiping like teenagers, but often when older siblings get together, they do just that.

_____

_____

3. For the most part, the favored kids recognize their status but keep quiet about it so the unfavored child doesn't complain too much.

_____

_____

4. More often than not, however, unfavored children whine and complain, even into adulthood, until their playing the role of the victim drives everyone crazy.

_____

_____

▲ How might these siblings compete for their parents' attention?

5. Children typically compete for their parents' attention by showing off as *the smart one*, or *the funny one*, or even *the naughty one*.

_____

2 Listening for Generalizations Read the statements below. Then listen to the lecture again, paying close attention to how the instructor uses the adverbs of time and other expressions to make generalizations. Mark the statements *T* (true) or *F* (false) as you listen. Listen to the lecture a second time, if necessary. When you are finished, compare your answers with a partner.

1. _____ In most cases, the longest relationships any of us will have are with our siblings.

▲ Normally, what might we expect the difference in longevity to be between a person and a dog?

2. _____ You typically know your siblings from the day you (or they) are born.

3. _____ Generally, you and your siblings can expect to live longer than your parents and certainly a lot longer than the average dog.

4. _____ Even though you may feel that your parents have a favorite child, parents really do love their children equally and seldom play favorites.

5. _____ For the most part, it is much better for a child to grow up in a home where there is no fighting or competition with siblings.

6. _____ In general, it would be best for your overall social development to actually be the favorite child rather than to be a less favored child.

7. _____ The assumption that siblings growing up in the same household will have similar impressions or memories of the same events or experiences is, more often than not, false.

8. _____ Regardless of their children's perceptions, parents typically do love their children equally.

9. _____ While in other cultures parents may be willing to admit they treated the eldest son best, this is not generally true in America with its emphasis on fairness and equality.

10. _____ Many family therapists claim that sibling rivalry, or competition, is normally a good thing.

3 Correcting False Statements Work with a partner to correct the false statements from Activity 2 and add appropriate facts.

Example

A false statement: ___F___ Even though you may feel that your parents have a favorite child, parents really do love their children equally and seldom play favorites.

Changed to a true statement:

Even though parents may say they love their children equally, we can often observe them playing favorites.

Supporting facts:

Researchers have shown that at least 65% of mothers and 70% of fathers exhibit a preference for one particular child.

True Statements (changed from Activity 2)	Supporting Facts
1.	
2.	
3.	
4.	

4 Using Generalizations Work in groups of four. Use the prompts below to discuss family dynamics in the community where you grew up. Use appropriate expressions for making generalizations as you discuss the following topics. Use at least nine different expressions and not just your favorites.

Example By and large, the average number of people in a household is...

- the number of people in a household
- the number of children in the average family
- the positive and negative effects of sibling rivalry
- reasons a sibling may become the favorite
- reasons a sibling may always remain close to siblings
- reasons a sibling may see siblings as "the enemy"
- the sibling most likely to become a politician
- the sibling most likely to become an extreme sports champion
- the person most likely to torment you
- the person who knows you best
- a common reason for low self-esteem and depression
- a common reason a favorite child fails later in life

PART 4 Focus on Testing

F☉CUS

TOEFL® iBT Pragmatic-Understanding Questions

When you listen for straw man arguments (as you did in this chapter), you try to accomplish a type of pragmatic understanding. You try to decide whether a speaker's statements are sincere or not. In this chapter you also developed your pragmatic language skills by listening for and making generalizations. On the TOEFL® iBT, pragmatic-understanding questions are asked not only about lectures but about conversations as well.

1 Pragmatic Understanding: Brief Informal Speeches In this chapter, you developed your pragmatic language skills by listening for and making generalizations. Listen to the brief informal speeches containing generalizations and answer the questions that follow.

1. **Speaker 1:** What is the speaker's main point?

   Ⓐ She loves David more than her other children.

   Ⓑ She wants Ruth and Alan to help David by doing his share of the work around the house this week.

   Ⓒ She thinks football is a very tiring game.

   Ⓓ She wants Ruth and Alan to take her and her husband out on Friday night.

2. **Speaker 2:** What is the man trying to say to his wife?

   (A) He's explaining why he doesn't call his son more often.

   (B) He's explaining why he wants to go see his grandchildren.

   (C) He's explaining why he doesn't feel comfortable visiting one of his children.

   (D) He's explaining why he doesn't get invited to his son's house.

2 Pragmatic Understanding: A Conversation Listen to the conversation between two friends. Close your books and take notes as you listen. Then open your books and answer the following pragmatic-understanding questions.

1. Listen again to part of the conversation.

   What does the man mean by saying, "No, no, it's OK"?

   (A) "It didn't really happen."

   (B) "No, you can't help."

   (C) "I don't mind saying."

   (D) "Nothing happened."

2. Why does the man mention the phone call?

   (A) to explain why he is late

   (B) to explain his problem

   (C) because he has nothing else to say

   (D) because he needs more time

3. Listen again to part of the conversation.

   Why does the man think the woman is cold?

   (A) She forgot to bring a sweater.

   (B) She doesn't seem to care that the man won't be able to see his father.

   (C) She does not like his father.

   (D) She needs more hot coffee.

4. Listen again to part of the conversation.

   Why does the woman mention the music concert?

   (A) to remind the man that he wanted to be a great musician

   (B) to remind the man that his brother couldn't go to the concert

   (C) to remind the man that he is holding on to a hurtful memory from his childhood

   (D) to remind the man that he had a terrible father

5. Why did the woman use straw man arguments throughout the conversation?

   (A) to make the man feel better about never seeing his father again

   (B) to help the man realize what a terrible father he has

   (C) to help the man understand that it might be time to forget about childhood hurts

   (D) to make sure that the man never speaks to his brother either

Self-Assessment Log

Check (✓) the words in this chapter you have acquired and can use in your daily life.

Nouns

- arrogance
- entitlement
- family dynamics
- household
- longevity
- siblings
- spouse
- statistics
- syndrome

Idiom

- miss the mark

Check (✓) your level of accomplishment for the skills introduced in this chapter. How comfortable do you feel using these skills?

	Very comfortable	Somewhat comfortable	Not at all comfortable
Listening for straw man arguments	☐	☐	☐
Doing research to check assumptions	☐	☐	☐
Understanding expressions such as *for the most part* and *hardly ever* when used to make generalizations	☐	☐	☐
Using expressions such as *for the most part* and *hardly ever* to make generalizations	☐	☐	☐

Think about the topics and activities in this chapter and complete the statements.

In this chapter, I learned something new about _____

_____

_____

I especially liked (topic or activity) _____

_____

_____

I would like to know more about _____

_____

_____

4 Health and Leisure

> "A man too busy
> to take care of his
> health is like a
> mechanic too busy
> to take care of his tools."
>
> Spanish proverb

In this
CHAPTER

Study Session Conversation What Makes Us Tick:
The Cardiac Muscle

Learning Strategy Understanding and Using Analogies

Language Function Expressing Opinions

Connecting to the Topic

1. What do people do during leisure time to keep their hearts healthy? List as many activities as you can.

2. Which of these activities do you do regularly? Once in a while?

3. Are there "downsides," or negative aspects, to any of these activities? What might they be?

Did You Know?

- An elephant's heart beats about 30 times per minute.
- The heart rate of a canary is about 1,000 beats per minute.
- Most people's hearts beat about 75 times a minute. However, this rate can go to over 175 beats a minute for a short time when the body is working hard.
- A clam's heart rate varies from two to 20 beats per minute.

1 **What Do You Think?** With a partner, do the following:

1. Discuss all of the things that you think make your heart beat faster.

2. Think about a time when your heart was really pounding. Take turns telling about this experience.

   - Where were you?
   - Who else was there?
   - Why was your heart pounding? What happened?

3. Discuss what you think a clam would be doing to get its heart rate to increase to 20 beats a minute (10 times the resting rate of two beats a minute).

Sharing Your Experience

2 **Making Some Comparisons** In what ways are parts of the human body like other things? With a partner, match the parts of the body in Column A to the items in Column B. Then pair up with another pair of students to discuss specifically how each body part is like the matched item.

◄ The eye could be compared to a camera because both automatically focus for short and long distances and adjust for lighting conditions.

A	B
1. _____ brain	**a.** scissors
2. __f__ eye	**b.** computer
3. _____ liver	**c.** crane
4. _____ nervous system	**d.** pump
5. _____ teeth	**e.** water filter
6. _____ arm	**f.** camera
7. _____ heart	**g.** electrical circuits

Vocabulary Preview

3 **Vocabulary in Context** The speakers in this chapter use the following words as they describe the heart. Complete the sentences with the correct forms of the vocabulary words.

Words	Definitions
cardiac muscles	*muscles of the heart*
chambers	*compartments*
hollow	*having an empty space inside*
peel	*the outside covering of some fruits, such as bananas*
pump	*to push or move a liquid through a system*
strip	*long, narrow piece*
tick-tock	*the sound a clock makes*
vary	*to change, differ*

1. The _____ in the heart fill with blood and empty over and over again as the heart works.

2. The _____ of the clock reminded Diana of her own heartbeat.

3. The doctor was concerned about the strength of Sue's _____ after her recent heart attack. He thought her heart might be weak.

4. The heart _____ blood through the entire body. The blood is continuously pulled in and pushed out of the heart.

5. Did you know that the _____ of an orange contains more vitamin C than the rest of the orange?

6. Francis used a _____ of cloth to make a bandage for his injured leg.

7. The size of an animal's heart _____ according to the size of the rest of its body. Large animals have large hearts while small animals have small hearts.

8. When the doctor tapped on the patient's stomach, it sounded

_____, as if there were nothing inside. The patient confirmed that he had not eaten anything at all in the last 24 hours.

Strategy

Listening for Analogies

When instructors explain a new concept, they will often compare the new idea to something that is already familiar to students. For example, the action of the heart might be compared to the action of a water pump. These kinds of comparisons are called *analogies*. Analogies that include the words *like* or *as* are called *similes*. A good analogy helps you to picture and remember a concept easily.

Expressions Used to Make Analogies

Expressions:	Examples:
as _____ as	The heart is as big as a fist.
(just) like	The heart works just like a pump.
similar to	The heartbeat is similar to a ticking clock.

Before You Listen

1 **Considering the Topic**   Before listening to the lecture, confirm and expand on what you know about the human heart.

- First, write down everything you already know about the heart in the chart below.
- In small groups, compare your notes with your classmates' notes and add any new information you hear in the column labeled "What I learned from my classmates."
- Then take turns visiting other groups to gather more information to write in the "What I learned..." column.

What I already know about the heart	What I learned from my classmates

2 **Listening for the "Gist" or Main Ideas** The students you will hear in the study session are reviewing their notes from a lecture on the heart. Listen to the study session once all the way through to get the "gist," or the main ideas of the conversation and to become accustomed to the voices of the speakers. Answer the following questions and then compare your answers with a classmate. Listen to the lecture again, if necessary.

1. Why are the students studying together?

2. What does one student do to settle a disagreement about the walls of the heart?

3. The rate of the heartbeat varies in relation to what?

4. What happens to a piece of the muscle of the heart when you cut it off and put it in a dish? What do the students say about why this happens?

5. What is the job of the heart?

3 **Listening for Analogies** Listen to the session again and complete the chart on page 66.

- Write down all the analogies you hear. You can write them in a short form by using the = sign.

  Example

  You hear: The eye is similar to a camera.

  You write: *eye = camera*

- Note which expressions the students use to make these analogies.
- When you are finished listening and have noted the analogies and which expressions the students use to make them, draw a simple picture or symbol to represent the analogy. It shouldn't be a detailed drawing, just something very simple that will help you to remember the analogy.

Item	Analogy	Expression Used	Drawing
shape of the heart	*heart = pear*	*similar to*	
walls of the heart			
strips of muscle at the bottom of the heart			
size of the heart			
beat of the heart			
action of the heart			

After You Listen

4 **Comparing Analogies** Share your list of analogies and expressions with your classmates. Discuss why these are or are not good analogies in your opinion. Remember: A good analogy helps you to picture and remember a concept easily. If necessary, listen to the study session again to hear the analogies your classmates had on their lists but that you missed.

Talk It Over

5 **Setting Contexts for Analogies** In small groups, discuss the analogies on page 67. Brainstorm together to come up with four or five situations in which each analogy could be used. When you are finished, share your lists with the rest of the class.

Example

His hand is shaking like a leaf.

Possible situations

He is at the dentist's office.
He is going to give a public talk for the first time.
He is trying to ask his girlfriend to marry him.
He is trying to explain to his girlfriend's father why he brought her home so late.

1. Her face is as white as a sheet.

_____

_____

_____

_____

_____

_____

2. He is as quiet as a mouse.

_____

_____

_____

_____

_____

_____

3. He is giving orders like an army general.

_____

_____

_____

_____

_____

_____

4. Her eyes are calm like a lake on a windless day.

_____

_____

_____

_____

_____

_____

6 **Discussing Analogies** Look at the list of analogies in the box. In small groups, discuss what these analogies might possibly mean. If you have absolutely no idea, use a dictionary or the Internet to discover how a particular analogy originated. Do you know of similar expressions in other languages? If so, explain them to your group in English and add them to the list. Share your results with the class.

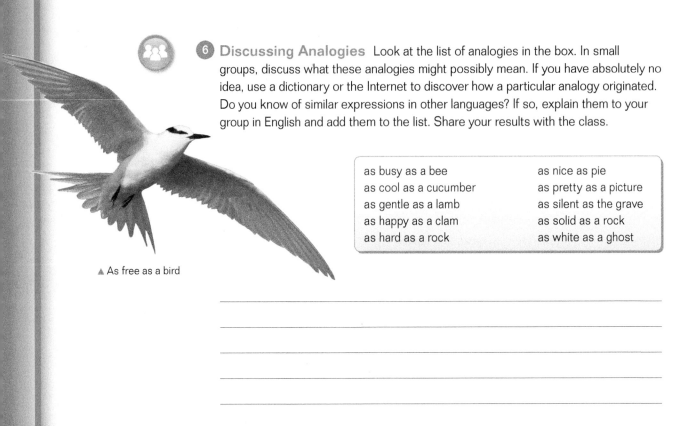

as busy as a bee	as nice as pie
as cool as a cucumber	as pretty as a picture
as gentle as a lamb	as silent as the grave
as happy as a clam	as solid as a rock
as hard as a rock	as white as a ghost

▲ As free as a bird

_____

_____

_____

_____

_____

PART 3 Expressing Opinions

Strategy

Introducing Your Opinion Appropriately

In the study session in this chapter, the speakers present a lot of factual information. In addition to these facts, the speakers express personal opinions. In general, when we express personal opinions, we don't want to seem like a "know-it-all" (a person who thinks he/she knows everything). We want to qualify, or soften, our remarks by using specific expressions to introduce them. These expressions also help the listener distinguish the facts from opinions.

Expressions Used to Introduce Personal Opinions

I'm convinced...	I (strongly) believe...	I think I'd say...
I'm fairly certain...	I bet...	In my opinion...
I'm (almost) positive...	I imagine...	Not everyone will agree with me, but...
I'm pretty sure...	I suspect...	

1 Recognizing a Know-It-All Listen to the following conversations in which Kenji and Paul express their opinions. Then answer the questions.

Conversation 1

1. Does Kenji express an opinion? _____

2. Does Paul express an opinion? _____

3. Does Paul indicate that his is a personal opinion?

_____

4. Which person sounds like a "know-it-all"? Why?

_____

_____

_____

_____

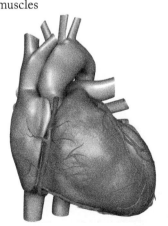

▲ When expressing personal opinions it's important not to sound like a know-it-all.

Conversation 2

What expressions does Paul use to introduce his personal opinions this time?

_____

_____

_____

2 Listening for Personal Opinions Listen to the study session again. Before you listen, read the numbered items below. Each item relates to an opinion. While you listen, focus on the expressions used to express opinions and add the missing information to each item, using your own words if you wish.

Example One student is convinced that the cardiac muscles are
         the most amazing muscles in the human body   .

1. Professor Miller is convinced that it is the action of the cardiac muscles

   that _____

   _____.

2. In Fred's opinion, the heart looks like _____

   _____.

3. Fred does not agree with the professor's analogy that the walls

   at the bottom of the heart are _____

   _____.

4. Greta is fairly certain that _____

   _____.

▲ The human heart

5. Ali is positive that Fred _____

_____.

6. Ali bets that scientists _____

_____ in ten or fifteen years.

7. Fred is pretty sure that Ali's heart _____

_____.

8. Fred thinks that Ali will _____

_____.

Talk It Over

3 **Expressing Personal Opinions** In small groups of at least five, discuss the following three situations. Use the expressions to introduce your personal opinions that you learned on page 68. If you wish, discuss other situations related to health as well.

Situation 1

The office workers in an insurance company did not do well on the yearly physical examination. They must decide what can be done to improve their physical fitness. They hold a meeting to discuss this.

Situation 2

Should health education be taught in school? If so, at what age (elementary, secondary, college) and in what class (biology, physical education)? A school meeting is held to discuss this issue.

Situation 3

In the United States, smoking is not allowed in classrooms, courthouses, and other public buildings. In fact, most American cities have passed laws banning smoking in places such as restaurants, bars, and shopping malls, and many companies have chosen to ban smoking in the workplace. A company is holding a meeting between the managers and employees to discuss whether to ban smoking in their workplace.

◀ In many U.S. cities, smoking is now prohibited in all public places.

4 **Role-Play** In the same groups, role-play the situations from Activity 3. Divide up the roles for each situation. Stay in character as you express the opinions of the character that you are role-playing. You may add, delete, or change characters as necessary to fit the size of your group. Choose one of the situations and perform it for the class.

Situation 1
Characters
the owner of the company
an extremely overweight accountant
the company doctor, a smoker
the company nurse, a vegetarian who eats healthy food
a young executive, a cyclist who rides her bike to work every day

Situation 2
Characters
a conservative parent
a broad-minded or liberal parent
a school principal
a high school senior
a counselor

Situation 3
Characters
an office worker who doesn't smoke but must work in a room with smokers
a college student who enjoys smoking
a pregnant woman
a person with lung disease
an elderly person who has smoked since the age of 15

F⊘CUS

Opinion Questions

Some of the speaking questions on the TOEFL® iBT ask your opinion about an issue. The expressions you studied in Part 3 of this chapter will be especially useful when answering this type of question.

1 **Pragmatic Understanding of Opinions: Brief Informal Speeches** Listen to these brief informal speeches and answer the following questions involving pragmatic understanding of opinions.

1. **Speaker 1:** What is the speaker implying?

    (A) We should pass more laws on smoking.

    (B) People have a right to smoke if they want to.

    (C) People dying of cancer should be allowed to eat where they want to.

    (D) People should quit smoking at home and smoke in restaurants instead.

2. **Speaker 2:** What does the speaker think?

    (A) She could win a bet on how much weight she can lose.

    (B) She is overweight, like most Americans.

    (C) She should lose 16 pounds.

    (D) Most people in America read newspapers.

2 **Expressing Opinions** Listen again to the study session conversation about the heart from Part 2 of this chapter. As you listen, close your books and take notes about the opinions expressed by the students. Then open your books and answer the following questions by speaking to another student. Use a variety of expressions to express your opinions. The audio gives you 30 seconds after each question to speak your answer.

1. Fred agrees with Professor Miller in some ways and disagrees in others in regards to what the heart looks like. Explain what each person thinks and then give your own opinion about the appearance of the heart.

2. What do the students agree to do to clarify a point they didn't understand from the lecture? Do you think this is the best way to handle this or do you have a better suggestion?

3. What does Ali think scientists will be able to tell us about the heart in the future? Do you think this is realistic? Why or why not?

4. What does Fred tease Ali about? Do you think that this is proper behavior among friends? Why or why not?

Self-Assessment Log

Check (✓) the words in this chapter you have acquired and can use in your daily life.

Nouns	Verbs	Adjective	Expression
cardiac muscles	pump	hollow	tick-tock
chambers	vary		
peel			
strip			

Check (✓) your level of accomplishment for the skills introduced in this chapter. How comfortable do you feel using these skills?

	Very comfortable	Somewhat comfortable	Not at all comfortable
Understanding expressions such as *similar to* when used to make analogies	☐	☐	☐
Using expressions such as *similar to* to make analogies	☐	☐	☐
Understanding expressions such as *I'm fairly certain, I bet,* and *I imagine* when used to express opinions	☐	☐	☐
Using expressions such as *I'm fairly certain, I bet,* and *I imagine* to express opinions	☐	☐	☐

Think about the topics and activities in this chapter and complete the statements.

In this chapter, I learned something new about _____

_____

_____

I especially liked (topic or activity) _____

_____

_____

I would like to know more about _____

_____

_____

CHAPTER 5

High Tech, Low Tech

"Space isn't remote at all. It's only an hour's drive away if your car could go straight upwards."

Fred Hoyle
British astronomer

In this
CHAPTER

Field Trip Spaceflight—A Simulation

Learning Strategy Taking Notes on a Field Trip

Language Function Shifting Between Active and
Passive Voice

 Connecting to the Topic

1 If you were a member of this space station crew, what would you
ask your project supervisor about your duties?

2 What would you ask the project dietician about meals?

3 What would you ask the project doctor about health and hygiene?

Did You Know?

- The success of high-tech projects sometimes depends on low-tech solutions. During a space mission to close the doors on the Hubble Space Telescope, all the astronauts' high-tech repair tools failed. They finally just gave up on the high-tech tools and forced the doors closed by hand.

- Astronauts F. Story Musgrave and Jeffrey Hoffman needed to replace Hubble's outdated camera with a new one. To protect the camera from damage by the sunlight, they did the job at night. For light they used the two flashlights on their helmets while the other astronauts on the shuttle shined their flashlights out the window.

- Often billions of dollars of equipment cannot do a job that a simple walk by two astronauts can accomplish. In one instance, space walks were used to replace a failed gyroscope and to restore power to another gyroscope on the International Space Station. The gyroscopes control the orientation, or position in space, of the station. After the astronauts completed their work by hand, all four of the station's gyroscopes were running simultaneously for the first time in three years.

▲ Making repairs in space can be both high-tech and low-tech.

① **What Do You Think?** Take turns speaking about the following with a partner.

1. Are you familiar with the International Space Station? What about a gyroscope, or the Hubble Space Telescope? Share your knowledge about these high-tech instruments.

2. What do the three situations above have in common? Why are they both amazing and amusing?

3. Share any other situations you know about where low-tech solutions came to the rescue and "saved the day."

2 Debating the Issue One of the reasons that the U.S. government chose to abandon its shuttle flights was because the manned space program was so expensive. Now astronauts and scientists must hitch rides on either the spaceships of other countries or those of private corporations in order to reach the International Space Station. In this activity, you will participate in a debate on the pros and cons of the privatization of space exploration and travel.

1. First, your instructor will split the class into two groups—Positions A and B. People for Position A will support the privatization of space travel. People for Position B will oppose the privatization. For the purposes of this activity, it doesn't matter what you actually believe about this issue.

   - **Position A (support privatization):** Work in groups of four to eight. Think of as many reasons as you can why the privatization of space travel is a great idea. Be sure to include reasons other than the obvious economic ones and list as many as you possibly can. Help each other prepare to speak clearly about this side of the issue. Be sure to take notes.

   - **Position B (oppose privatization of space travel):** Work in groups of four to eight. Think of reasons why space travel should not be privatized. Be sure to list as many reasons as you possibly can. Help each other prepare to speak clearly about this side of the issue. Be sure to take notes.

   Notes

   _____

   _____

   _____

2. When you are finished working in your groups, your teacher will put you in groups of four. Each group will have two people for Position A and two for Position B. In these new groups, debate the issue until your instructor calls, "Time's up!"

3. Share how the debates went in each group with the whole class.

▲ British billionaire Richard Branson poses in front of a model of the Virgin Galactic, the world's first commercial spaceline.

3 **Vocabulary in Context** The words in the following list are used in the guided simulation of a spaceflight in this chapter. Complete the sentences with the correct forms of the vocabulary words. **Note:** not all of the words are used.

Words	Definitions
acceleration	the process of increasing speed
altitude	the distance above sea level
astronaut	a person who is trained to fly or be a crew member on a spacecraft
atmosphere	the air surrounding Earth
cargo bay	an area in an airplane or spaceship used to keep cargo, special goods, or materials
friction	the rubbing of one thing against another; resistance to motion by two surfaces that are touching
manipulate	to control
mission	a special job or assignment given to a person or group
orbit	the circular path one body makes around another body in space (such as the moon around Earth)
orbiter	a vehicle or thing that orbits
remote	distant, far
satellite	an object or vehicle that orbits Earth or another body in space
shuttle (n.)	a vehicle used to shuttle
shuttle (v.)	to travel back and forth frequently
simulate	to copy the appearance or effect of something
solar	of or about the sun

1. _____ need a lot of training before they can pilot a spaceship.

2. Although the scientist was on Earth and the spaceship was 690 miles above Earth, it was his _____ to repair the ship by _____ control.

3. In their training, astronauts use devices and instruments that _____ spaceflights. This training helps astronauts learn what a real spaceflight will be like.

4. The horrified pilot found it was impossible to _____ the navigational instruments in order to steer the plane.

5. The suitcases were held in the _____ of the plane.

6. As a spaceship falls toward Earth and enters Earth's _____ at an _____ of 400,000 feet, a great deal of resistance, or _____, builds up between the shuttle and the atmosphere.

7. They launched a communication _____ into

   _____ around the moon.

8. There is a bus that will _____ passengers from the airport parking lot to the terminals.

9. On the outside of the spacecraft, there are _____ panels, which collect the energy from the sun.

10. As the rockets fired, the spaceship sped faster and faster toward the sky.

    The _____ of the spaceship pushed the pilots into their seats.

PART **2** Taking Notes on a Field Trip

Strategy

Hints for Taking Notes on Field Trips

1. Before the field trip, get as much information as possible about the place you are going to visit. The more you already know, the easier it will be for you to understand your guide. You can read a book, do an online search, look in an encyclopedia, or talk to other students who have been on a similar field trip.
2. During the field trip, write down important numbers such as measurements, years, and amounts of things. If you don't have time to write down all the information concerning the numbers, you can ask the guide or your instructor to help you fill in the missing information later.
3. After the field trip, share notes with a classmate. You probably won't be able to write down every important thing, and each of you may have written down different important facts.

FYI

Field trips are real-world educational experiences designed by an instructor. It is often very difficult to take good notes on a field trip because so much information is presented while you are also dealing with the distractions (noise and movement) of a real-world setting.

Before You Listen

1 **Using the Internet** Before listening to the spaceflight simulation from a field trip to a space center, use the Internet to find information about space travel.

- Write down at least five facts and share them in class in small groups.
- See which group found the most information (no repetitions) and the most interesting or surprising information.

2 Discussing the Handout Before the spaceflight simulation, the guide at the space center hands out a diagram of the phases of the space mission. Look at the following diagram and the list of coded headings. With a partner, discuss which code might match each picture in the diagram.

T = Tower

OCB = Opening Cargo Bay

D = Deorbit

EF = Engines Fire

BR = Booster Rockets Drop Away

EO = Enter Orbit (altitude 690 miles)

ET = External Tank Drops Away

L = Landing

RMA = Using Remote Manipulation Arm

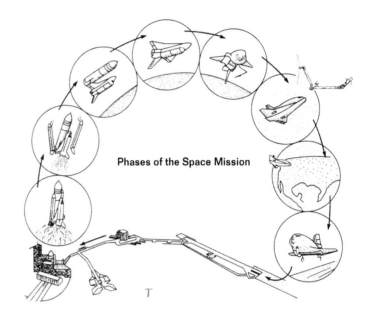

Phases of the Space Mission

3 Taking Notes

1. Listen to the simulation. Listen for the major points about the phases of the mission. As you hear about each phase of the mission in space, confirm or correct your code for each picture in the diagram above in Activity 2.

2. Listen again to the simulation. Take notes about the Remote Manipulation Arm. Draw or write notes on the following diagram of the arm.

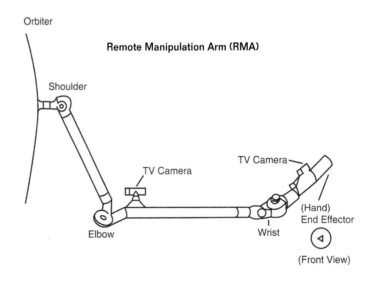

Orbiter

Remote Manipulation Arm (RMA)

Shoulder

TV Camera

TV Camera

(Hand)
End Effector

Elbow

Wrist

(Front View)

4 Listening for Measurements and Amounts Now that you have a clearer idea of the technical vocabulary used in the simulation, it will be easier to concentrate on the numbers and statistics.

1. Practice saying the following numbers aloud with a partner. Make sure you can each identify the numbers spoken.

10	= ten	1/2	= one-half
100	= one hundred	1/3	= one-third
1,000	= one thousand	1/4	= one-fourth
10,000	= ten thousand	1/5	= one-fifth
100,000	= one hundred thousand	1/6	= one-sixth
1,000,000	= one million	1/7	= one-seventh
10,000,000	= ten million	1/8	= one-eighth
100,000,000	= one hundred million	1/9	= one-ninth
1,000,000,000	= one billion	1/10	= one-tenth
		1/20	= one-twentieth

2. Read the following items. Listen to the simulation again and complete the sentences. When you are finished, review your answers with a partner or in small groups.

1. The spaceship's acceleration builds up to four times the speed of sound, or _____ feet per second as we move away from Earth.

2. The booster rockets use up their fuel and drop into the sea about _____ minutes after takeoff.

3. As the spaceship heads into orbit, its speed is _____ times the speed of sound.

4. When the spaceship is in orbit, it flies at an altitude of _____ miles.

5. The _____-foot mechanical arm attached to the orbiter is called the RMA.

6. The hand, or what is called the *end effector* of the RMA, has _____ wires inside.

7. The shuttle enters Earth's atmosphere at an altitude of _____ feet.

8. When the shuttle enters Earth's atmosphere, it is _____ miles from its landing site.

9. As the orbiter reaches Earth's atmosphere, its surface temperature can reach _____ degrees Fahrenheit.

10. As the engines shut off, the orbiter continues to come down to Earth at _____ feet per minute.

▲ Takeoffs and landings are notoriously the most dangerous parts of spaceflights.

After You Listen

5 **Using Notes to Recall Information** Working in small groups, take turns using your notes on the diagrams of the mission phases and the Remote Manipulation Arm to describe the phases of the mission and the use of the RMA.

Talk It Over

6 **Taking Notes on Other Topics**

1. Work with a partner. Think of a city or town that you are very familiar with and enjoy visiting. Give your partner a talking "mini-tour" of this city or town while he or she takes careful notes and asks questions as needed for clarification. (As an alternative, you may take your partner on a "mini-tour" of someplace other than a town—for example, a college, a factory, a vacation spot, or another place that you know well.) Here are some types of information you might want to include in your tour:

   • points of historical interest
   • shopping areas
   • museums
   • city or town hall

- tourist attractions, such as amusement parks, zoos, and theaters
- schools and universities
- geographical attractions (lakes, rivers, mountains)
- transit systems

2. Now switch places. Listen and take notes while your partner gives you a talking "mini-tour" of his or her chosen town or place. Take careful notes and ask questions for clarification.

3. Using the notes you took during your partner's mini-tour as a guide, present a two- or three-minute report to the class about your partner's town or place.

PART **3** Shifting Between Active and Passive Voice

Strategy

Distinguishing Between Active and Passive Voice

As you have heard in the listening selections, instructors often use "academic English," which is impersonal and formal. To create a feeling of objectivity, they may use the passive voice. Here are some hints to help you recognize the passive voice and to help you compare it with the active voice.

- A verb in the passive voice consists of a form of the verb *to be* plus a past participle.

    Example   The shuttle **was flown.**

- Sometimes in sentences using the passive voice, the doer of the action is mentioned, but is not as important as the subject of the sentence.

    S   V   doer
    Example   The shuttle was flown by a pilot.

    Notice the use of the word *by* and the impersonal tone of the sentence.

- In contrast, in sentences using the active voice, the doer is the subject of the sentence and the focus of attention.

    S = doer V   O
    Example   My aunt flew the shuttle.

    Notice that the sentence contains a personal reference. It does not have the same neutral, impersonal tone of a passive voice sentence. In fact, in this example the speaker could even be bragging a little.

1 **Contrasting the Passive and Active Voice** In the following pairs of conversations, the active voice is contrasted with the passive voice, and the personal is contrasted with the impersonal. Listen to each pair of conversations and answer the questions.

Conversation 1
Two astronauts are discussing the effects of a hurricane.

Conversation 2
Two astronauts are discussing how they feel about launch delays.

---

1. Which conversation (1 or 2) contains the passive voice? _____

2. Why do you think the passive voice was used in this situation?

_____

Conversation 3
A space travel project engineer and a project supervisor are discussing a problem.

Conversation 4
The space travel project supervisor is telling a news reporter what happened.

---

1. Which conversation (3 or 4) contains the passive voice? _____

2. Why do you think the passive voice was used in this situation?

_____

▼ Mission Control Center

> **Conversation 5**
> A husband and wife are in their living room talking.
>
> **Conversation 6**
> The woman is on the phone with an electric company employee.

1. Which conversation (5 or 6) contains the passive voice? _____

2. Why do you think the passive voice was used in this situation?

   _____

 2 **Listening for the Passive Voice** Read the following incomplete sentences. The sentences are all in the passive voice and appear in the order in which they occur in the spaceflight simulation. Listen to the simulation once more. Complete the sentences with the correct forms of the verbs in parentheses.

1. At T minus zero, the two booster rockets fire, and three seconds later we

   _____ (lift) off the ground by the combined energy of the

   five engines.

2. Two minutes after takeoff, the
   fuel in the booster rockets

   _____ (use up).

3. Since the failure of its control
   system, the satellite has been moving
   through space without guidance—
   moving so fast that it cannot

   _____ (reach)

   directly by the Remote Manipulation

   Arm.

4. The hand, or what

   _____ (call) the

   end effector, _____

   _____ (fit)

   with three inside wires.

5. A short arm of the satellite

   _____ (catch)

   by these wires.

▲ Sometimes just doing it by hand is the only solution.

6. Remember, we said that the satellite was moving too quickly

_____ (pick up) directly by the RMA.

7. This is Mission Control. Congratulations! Your mission

_____ (accomplish).

8. However, we _____ (protect) from surface temperatures of

2,750 degrees Fahrenheit by the thermal tiles covering the ship.

9. The heat is so great that our radio communications _____

(cut off) for 12 minutes on our descent.

Talk It Over

1 Using the Passive Voice to Report the News Here are some "facts" about an imaginary accident at a private spaceflight company. In small groups, take turns completing sentences 1–14 of the report, using the passive voice and the cues provided. Note that the events are in chronological order and occurred in the past as indicated in sentences A and B. You may add additional items.

FYI

Radio and TV announcers try to remain impersonal and detached from the stories they report; therefore, the passive voice is often used in news reporting.

A. Yesterday there was a tragic fire after a liftoff on launch pad number 2.

1. the astronauts / give

2. the countdown / begin

3. the astronauts / ask

4. the controls / check

5. all systems / test

6. the signal / give

B. Suddenly a fire broke out in the booster rockets before the spaceship took off.

7. the astronauts' cabin / fill

8. the fire / put out

9. the pilots / kill

10. two mechanics / injure

11. Flight Control personnel / shock

12. burned pieces / find

13. the public / inform

14. the next flight / cancel

4 **Role-Playing a News Reporter** Consider an event that you have experienced or witnessed (or you may listen to a radio or TV news report and take notes). Present this event to the class in the style of a news report. You may make this report either humorous or serious, but be sure to use the passive voice to create an impersonal tone.

F⊙CUS

TOEFL® iBT

Note-Taking for Standardized Tests

When you take notes on listening passages for the TOEFL® iBT, you have to organize them as efficiently as you can right from the start. You will have no chance to organize them later or to ask other students about points you may have missed.

One good strategy is to guess from the beginning about possible relationships of ideas in the listening passage. A good guess can help you organize sections in your notes to make those relationships clear.

For example, a lecture that starts, "Today we're going to look at some low-tech forms of weather damage control and why they work…" is likely to (1) list some weather damage-control methods and (2) describe the operation of each one. If your notes have a column on the left for listing methods and a column on the right to make notes about the operation of each one, your job will be a lot easier. It would also be smart to leave an open column on the left or the right for any extra details about each method.

Another good strategy is to take advantage of TOEFL® iBT questions that replay part of the lecture or conversation. This gives you a chance to quickly check part of your notes and make changes if necessary.

1 **Note-Taking Practice** Listen to the following conversation between a guide at a science museum and some visiting students. Be ready to take notes in two columns (main ideas and explanations or details). Listen for organization clues at the beginning of the passage. After you've finished taking notes, use them to answer the following questions.

1. Listen again to part of the exchange.

   Which of the following does the tour guide most strongly imply about low-tech solutions?

   (A) They are humorous.

   (B) They cause problems.

   (C) They are simple.

   (D) They are complicated.

2. According to the tour guide, what item in the exhibit was fixed by using aluminum foil?

   (A) part of a car

   (B) a sound system

   (C) part of a pot

   (D) a satellite dish

3. Listen again to part of the exchange.

   Why, according to the tour guide, was the solution involving gum especially helpful to the clarinetist?

   (A) It was more permanent than other repair methods.

   (B) It was less expensive than other repair methods.

   (C) It was more highly sophisticated than other repair methods.

   (D) It could be used more quickly than other repair methods.

4. Listen again to part of the exchange.

   Which of the following is most likely to come next in the tour?

   (A) an exhibit about butter knives

   (B) an exhibit about shaking things

   (C) an exhibit that plays a DVD

   (D) an exhibit about electricity

Self-Assessment Log

Check (✓) the words in this chapter you have acquired and can use in your daily life.

Nouns		Verbs	Adjectives
▨ acceleration	▨ mission	▨ manipulate	▨ remote
▨ altitude	▨ orbit	▨ shuttle	▨ solar
▨ astronaut	▨ orbiter	▨ simulate	
▨ atmosphere	▨ satellite		
▨ cargo bay	▨ shuttle		
▨ friction			

Check (✓) your level of accomplishment for the skills introduced in this chapter. How comfortable do you feel using these skills?

	Very comfortable	Somewhat comfortable	Not at all comfortable
Taking notes on a field trip	☐	☐	☐
Listening for active and passive voice	☐	☐	☐
Shifting between active and passive voice	☐	☐	☐

Think about the topics and activities in this chapter and complete the statements.

In this chapter, I learned something new about _____
_____
_____

I especially liked (topic or activity) _____
_____
_____

I would like to know more about _____
_____
_____

6 Money Matters

"Only after the last
tree has been cut down,
Only after the last
river has been poisoned,
Only after the last fish
has been caught,
Only then will you find that
money cannot be eaten."

Cree Indian prophecy
Native Americans, United States

In this **CHAPTER**

Radio Program The World Bank Under Fire

Learning Strategy Understanding and Constructing Pro and Con Arguments

Language Function Agreeing and Disagreeing

Connecting to the Topic

1. What does the Native American prophecy on the facing page mean to you? Do you have a similar saying in your native language?

2. What do you think this saying means? *If you look after the pennies, the dollars will look after themselves.*

3. Do you agree or disagree with this saying? *An investment in knowledge always pays the best interest.*

4. Have you ever met anyone like the person in this saying? *Someone who has the opinion that money will do everything, may well be suspected of doing everything for money.*

Did You Know?

- From 2007–2011, a branch of the World Bank called the International Bank for Reconstruction and Development (IBRD) lent $142 billion to these ten countries (in order of total amount borrowed): India, China, Brazil, Mexico, Pakistan, Turkey, Indonesia, Bangladesh, Argentina, and Vietnam.

- The International Development Association (IDA), the World Bank's lower interest lending branch, provides funding to the poorer member nations. Over $100 billion is still owed by borrowing nations.

- Most of the money loaned by the World Bank is used for transportation, law, justice, health, and public administration projects.

- Many people disagree with some of the projects the World Bank helps support. For example, they question the value of building a dam to provide water for crops when it leaves thousands of people homeless and destroys forests along with endangered plants and animals.

1 **What Do You Think?** Which are more valuable: modern conveniences or natural resources? Imagine you live in a village that will be flooded when a new dam is built to provide electric power to the region. In pairs, discuss and note what you think are the pros and cons, the advantages and disadvantages, of such an action.

Pros	Cons

2 What Do You Know About Banks? What are the different kinds of services that banks perform? In small groups, share as many services as you can think of and write them on the lines of the sunray diagram below. Add extra lines if you need them. When you are finished, share your ideas with other groups in order to compile (put together) one complete list for the class.

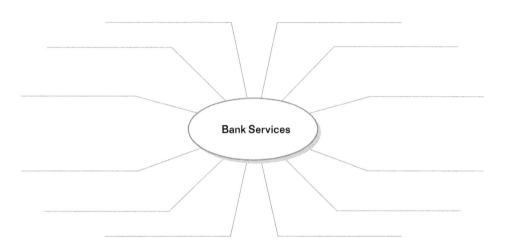

Bank Services

3 What Do You Think About Banks? Are banks friends or enemies? Discuss the following questions in small groups. Then share the highlights of your discussions with the whole class.

1. Banks may be seen as friends in a time of need. For instance, when the owner of a small business wants to expand, he or she may go to the bank for a loan. On the other hand, banks may be seen as enemies in a time of hardship. For example, if a family can't pay the mortgage on their home, the bank may foreclose and take ownership of the property. Think of a person or family who has been helped or hurt by a bank. What did the bank do? How did this affect the people involved?

2. Can you think of a business that depends on a bank for its operation? What does the bank do for the business? Try to describe ways that the bank has helped or hurt this company.

▲ Getting a loan is sometimes the only way to buy a house or get a business started.

4 Crossword Puzzle The following vocabulary items are from a radio program on the World Bank that you will hear in this chapter. Read the definitions and use the correct forms of the words to complete the crossword puzzle. Compare your answers with a partner. (Answers are on page 215.)

Words	Definitions
alleviate	*to lessen or make easier*
borrow	*to take something with permission (with the intention of returning it)*
breed	*to mate or reproduce*
environmental	*relating to the living conditions experienced by plants, animals, and people*
insiders	*people in a group or organization who have special knowledge of how it works*
invest	*to put money into a project in order to earn more money*
irrigation	*watering of farmland by canals, ditches, and so on*
loan	*to give something with the intention of getting it back*
proposal	*a suggestion (either spoken or presented as a written plan)*
snail	*a simple creature with a soft, wet body in a coiled shell*
under fire	*under attack; needing defense*

Across

1. Rabbits and mice do this rapidly.

2. What you do when you need money.

3. Dry lands need this in order to produce food.

4. Sometimes money can _____ the problems of the poor.

5. Some people eat them.

Down

1. Air and water pollution problems are _____ problems.

2. You hope that the bank will _____ you money.

3. What business people often study before making decisions.

4. These people are "in the know."

5. A financial advisor will tell you how to _____ your money.

6. She really defended her position well when she was under _____.

Strategy

Expressing Pros and Cons

Speakers often state arguments for (pros) and arguments against (cons) the points they are making. To call attention to both the pro and the con arguments, a speaker uses words that indicate a switch from one point of view to the other. For example:

> "Now is definitely the time to buy into this company. It's just beginning to grow so you can buy shares at a very good price. However, the company could grow too quickly and not be able to manage this growth well. In that case, you could lose some money."

After telling why it's a good idea to invest in the company (giving a pro argument), the speaker uses the word *however* to introduce some negative information (a con argument). Following are some linking expressions you can use when you want to express both a pro and a con argument for something.

Expressions Used to Link Pros and Cons

although	however	nonetheless	on the other hand
but	instead	on the contrary	

Before You Listen

1 **Matching Up Pro and Con Arguments** Match the "pro" argument on the left with the appropriate "con" argument on the right.

Pros

1. Borrowing money from a bank can help you start a new business.

2. Working while in school may help you avoid student loan debt.

3. Some people buy whatever new technological "toy" they want, such as video cameras and the latest TVs.

4. It's tempting to sign up for every credit card offer in the mail when you have a lot of bills to pay.

5. Some economists predict that stock prices will go up this year.

Cons

_____ Instead, it would be much better if they saved some of their money for retirement.

_____ On the contrary, they could just as easily go down.

_____ On the other hand, this might leave very little time to study.

_____ However, it can also put you into debt if the business fails.

_____ Nonetheless, you will be better off having only one credit card in the long run.

2 **Formulating Challenging Questions** You are going to listen to a radio program called "The World Bank Under Fire." Michelle Barney, the radio station's financial reporter, interviews a guest, Mr. George Cruz from the World Bank, and asks some very challenging questions.

- In small groups, come up with at least six questions that you would like to ask Mr. Cruz about the World Bank. Write them in the chart below.
- Share your questions as a whole class and add any new and interesting questions you hear to your list.
- In Activity 5, you will have a chance to come back to your questions here and discuss whether they were answered by the speaker satisfactorily or not.

Questions about the World Bank	Answered satisfactorily? Why?	Not answered satisfactorily? Why?

3 Listening for Pros and Cons Now you will listen to a radio program about the World Bank that covers many pros and cons of three World Bank agencies. Look carefully at the chart on page 98 before you begin.

1. Listen to the program once all the way through to get the gist or main ideas of the interview and to become familiar with the voices and mannerisms of the speakers.

2. Listen again to the first part of the lecture, covering the pros and cons of the International Bank for Reconstruction and Development (IBRD). Complete the first column (IBRD) in the chart as you listen. You may need to listen several times.

3. Listen again to the next part of the interview covering the pros and cons of the International Development Association (IDA) and complete the second column (IDA) in the chart. Listen a few times, if necessary.

4. Listen again to the part of the interview covering the pros and cons of the International Finance Corporation (IFC) and complete the third column (IFC) in the chart. Listen a few times, if necessary.

▲ Sometimes countries borrow money in order to provide clean water.

Member Agencies of the World Bank		
International Bank for Reconstruction and Development (IBRD)	International Development Association (IDA)	International Finance Corporation (IFC)
Pros (advantages)	Pros (advantages)	Pros (advantages)
1.	1.	1.
2.	2.	2.
3.	3.	3.
Cons (disadvantages)	Cons (disadvantages)	Cons (disadvantages)
1.	1.	1.
2.	2.	2.
3.	3.	3.

After You Listen

4 Comparing Pros and Cons Compare your chart on the pros and cons of the three World Bank agencies with your classmates. Discuss any differences in your charts.

5 Reviewing Your Questions In small groups, return to the questions you wrote for the Formulating Challenging Questions activity on page 96. Were your questions answered satisfactorily during the radio program? Discuss why or why not.

Talk It Over

6 Considering Ways to Invest Your Money In the chart on page 99 are some possible ways to invest money. In small groups, write this list in large print on poster paper. Then:

- Take turns adding suggestions of other ways to invest money until your instructor says, "Time's up."
- Use markers to draw symbols representing the type of investment next to each suggestion, so that they can be easily seen across the room.
- Hang up your posters and share your suggestions with the whole class.

Symbol	Investment Suggestions
	Buy an apartment. Rent it now and sell it later at a profit.
	Buy individual stocks on the stock market.
	Buy 1,000 lottery tickets for $1.00 each.

$$$
Guaranteed Rates
for the
Serious Investor

INVESTMENT CERTIFICATES

$10,000 "Mini Jumbo"		
TERM	RATE	YIELD
3 MONTHS	3.25	3.29
6 MONTHS	3.60	3.67
12 MONTHS	3.92	4.00

$100,000 "Giant Jumbo"		
TERM	RATE	YIELD
3 MONTHS	3.35	3.39
6 MONTHS	3.60	3.67
12 MONTHS	3.95	4.03

$10,000 minimum investment on "Mini Jumbo" and
$100,000 minimum investment on "Giant Jumbo."
Penalty for early withdrawl. Available to California
residents only.
Interest paid monthly or deposited to passbook account.
(LIMITED OFFER)

FIRESIDE *Thrift*

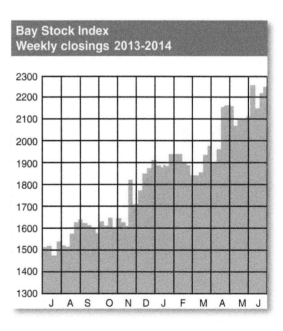

Bay Stock Index
Weekly closings 2013-2014

7 **Discussing Pros and Cons of Investments** Working in small groups, discuss the pros and cons of the investment ideas on the posters displayed around the class. In the chart below, list as many pros and cons as the group can think of for each unique type of investment. Use additional paper as needed. Examine your group's list of pros and cons carefully. Then take a vote on which investment your group thinks is the best. Report the results of the voting to the rest of the class.

Investment Suggestion	Pros	Cons

Strategy

Agreeing and Disagreeing Confidently, Yet Politely
Often in schools, colleges, and universities in the United States and other English-speaking countries, when instructors give a point of view, they expect students to react to their statements by agreeing or disagreeing. Expressing your own point of view is valued as independent thinking. Of course, being able to agree or disagree is valuable outside, as well as inside, the classroom. Every day most of us are asked to give our points of view in conversations with friends, relatives, and acquaintances.

To feel comfortable when we express our points of view, we need to know the vocabulary of agreeing and disagreeing. We also need to know which expressions are polite and which are not.

Expressions for Expressing Agreement

Informal	Formal
Absolutely!	Exactly.
I know what you mean.	I agree with that.
I'll say!	I agree.
That's for sure!	I couldn't agree more!
That's/You're right.	That's (absolutely) true!
You can say that again!	That's precisely the point!
You'd better believe it!	That's/You're correct!

Expressions for Expressing Disagreement

Informal*	Formal (assertive, may be heard as aggressive)
That's a laugh!	I don't think so at all.
That's a joke!	I'm afraid not.
You don't know what	I'm sorry, but I disagree.
you're talking about!	I'm sorry, but I don't agree.
You've got to be joking!	I'm sorry, but I don't believe that.
You've got to be kidding!	No, definitely not!
	You couldn't be more wrong!

Formal (polite)

I guess that's true, but...
I guess you could say that, but...
I understand what you mean, but...
That's more or less true, but...
Yes, but isn't it also true that...?

*NOTE: To avoid sounding rude, the informal expressions should be used with a sincere, friendly
tone and only with friends, never with strangers.

1 **Listening for Appropriate Uses of Expressions** Listen to the following
conversations in which expressions of agreement and disagreement are used both
appropriately and inappropriately. Then answer the questions.

Conversation 1

In a college classroom, a student is challenging an instructor.

1. Do you think the student is being polite or rude? _____

2. Why? _____

Conversation 2

Now listen to a different student respond to the same instructor.

1. Do you think this student responded appropriately? _____

2. Why or why not? _____

Conversation 3

Two students are chatting in the school cafeteria.

Paul probably doesn't have too many friends. Why do you think this might be?

_____

Conversation 4

Let's give Paul another chance to respond to Roger a bit more appropriately.

Why is the expression that Paul uses this time to agree with Roger more

appropriate? _____

Conversation 5

At a corporation meeting, two board members are discussing future plans.

1. Do you think these board members will reach an agreement easily? _____

2. Why or why not? _____

Conversation 6

Now listen to two other board members in a similar conversation.

1. How is this conversation different from the previous one?

   _____

   _____

2. Do you think these board members will be able to reach an agreement more
   or less easily than the board members in the previous conversation? Why?

   _____

   _____

Conversation 7

At the doctor's office, a doctor is discussing her patient, a 12-year-old boy, with
the boy's mother, Mrs. Franklin.

1. Is Mrs. Franklin agreeing or disagreeing with the doctor? _____

2. Is Mrs. Franklin responding formally or informally? _____

Conversation 8

Listen to the doctor and Mrs. Franklin again. This time Mrs. Franklin responds
differently.

1. Is Mrs. Franklin responding formally or informally? _____

2. Which of Mrs. Franklin's responses do you think is more appropriate—the
   response she gives in Conversation 7 or the one she gives in Conversation 8?
   Why?

   _____

   _____

2 Agreeing and Disagreeing Listen to the radio program again. This time your instructor will stop the recording ten times so that you can practice with a partner using appropriate expressions to agree or disagree with the speaker.

- Use the list of expressions from the list on page 101.
- When you agree with a point, give your reason, and support your idea with an example from your own experience if possible.
- When you disagree, give your reason.
- Before listening, read the following sentences with your partner. They will be the last sentences you hear before your instructor stops the recording, so it is important that you understand them.

Stop 1: But it turns out that money isn't everything.

Stop 2: The critics of the World Bank say that this kind of help to developing countries is wasteful, destructive, and unfair.

Stop 3: Isn't it true that in some cases, developing countries have been forced to cut spending on health, education, transportation, and welfare programs in order to reduce their huge debts to the World Bank?

Stop 4: Well, this rule is good for the countries and companies that want to sell goods to developing countries, but wouldn't this discourage local production of goods?

Stop 5: … we know that technological advances can sometimes cause environmental problems.

Stop 6: … understanding local needs and culture may be more important than anything else in the success of a project.

Stop 7: … this is how member nations can dictate what governmental policies must be in place before loans will be given…

Stop 8: This is good for the country because the government does not have to guarantee the loan and it encourages the growth of private business and industry.

Stop 9: … the loan is more effective if people in the region spend the money in ways they think are best…

Stop 10: But we all know that it is difficult to separate economic goals from political interests in today's world.

▲ Many countries apply for loans to fund public health projects.

3 **Agreeing and Disagreeing with Items in the News** In this activity, you will have the opportunity to practice expressions for agreeing and disagreeing while discussing current events. First, find a newspaper, magazine, or online article that you feel strongly about and bring a copy to class. Summarize the major issue in the article for the class. Then, state the author's point of view and explain why you agree or disagree.

Talk It Over

4 **Planning for Economic Prosperity** In this activity, you will come up with a plan to help a country called "Potential Prosperity."

1. As a whole class, read aloud the following information about the struggling country of Potential Prosperity and ask for explanations of any concepts you don't understand.

2. Work in groups of five or six. Each group should come up with at least five actions that could be taken to improve the economic conditions in Potential Prosperity. Write them on poster paper. Use markers to draw pictures to clarify or symbolize your ideas.

3. Hang up the posters. Each group should take turns standing next to its poster and reporting its suggestions for action.

4. After each group is finished, the members of other groups should say whether they agree or disagree with each suggestion and why.

Be sure to use the expressions of agreement and disagreement presented in this chapter. Begin with practicing use of the formal expressions. Then as the discussion continues, use the more informal expressions making sure to use an appropriate tone of voice.

The Land of Potential Prosperity has:

abundant natural resources (recently discovered): oil, uranium
a common language (spoken by all)
several large towns
several large rivers flowing from the mountains
a large lake
a pleasant climate
a mountainous central region
no outlet to the sea (is landlocked)

only one major export
imports that greatly exceed exports
a high unemployment rate
a high illiteracy rate
a high inflation rate
poor soil
a large population
a low minimum hourly wage
unfriendly neighboring countries

The Land of Potential Prosperity

FOCUS

TOEFL® iBT

Making Inferences

The TOEFL® iBT places a lot of emphasis on *making inferences*. This is an ability to understand what a speaker is saying by "reading between the lines" or to understand what is said indirectly in order to see what logical conclusions, opinions, or effects can be inferred from or are implied in the information given. Making inferences is important when a speaker does not reveal information, attitudes, opinions, strategies, or goals by stating them directly. When you learned in this chapter about listening for pros and cons, you were also learning to make inferences from what is being said.

1 **Making Inferences: Brief Conversations** Listen to these brief conversations and answer the inference questions that follow.

Conversation 1

What is the woman implying?

(A) Banks are loaning less money to people with low incomes than in the past.

(B) There are pros and cons to accepting bank loans.

(C) The bank gives away money to the poor.

(D) Banks use string to tie up sacks of money.

Conversation 2

What is the woman implying? (choose two)

(A) Don't agree with me without thinking it through.

(B) I don't agree with you.

(C) It can take years to save enough money to buy something.

(D) You will save money if you pay cash for something.

2 **Making Inferences: Radio Program** Listen to the radio program in this chapter about the World Bank again. Close your books as you listen and take notes about what can be inferred from or is implied in what is being said. Then open your books and answer the following questions by speaking to another student. Use a variety of expressions to convey your opinions or the pros and cons of an issue. The audio gives you 30 seconds after each question to speak your answer.

1. Listen to a part of the radio program again.

   What is the speaker implying?

2. Listen to a part of the radio program again.

   What is the speaker inferring about Mr. Cruz?

3. Listen to a part of the radio program again.

   What is Mr. Cruz inferring about Ms. Barney's attitude toward the World Bank?

4. Listen to a part of the radio program again.

   What is Mr. Cruz inferring about World Bank projects in the future?

5. Overall, what do you think Mr. Cruz is implying about local needs and culture in relation to both past and future World Bank projects?

6. Listen to a part of the radio program again.

   What is Mr. Cruz implying about the ideals of Robert McNamara?

Self-Assessment Log

Check (✓) the words in this chapter you have acquired and can use in your daily life.

Nouns	Verbs	Adjective	Idiom
▦ insiders	▦ alleviate	▦ environmental	▦ under fire
▦ irrigation	▦ borrow		
▦ proposal	▦ breed		
▦ snail	▦ invest		
	▦ loan		

Check (✓) your level of accomplishment for the skills introduced in this chapter. How comfortable do you feel using these skills?

	Very comfortable	Somewhat comfortable	Not at all comfortable
Listening for pros and cons	☐	☐	☐
Using expressions such as *although* and *nonetheless* to discuss pros and cons	☐	☐	☐
Understanding expressions such as *I'll say!* and *I couldn't agree more!* when used to agree	☐	☐	☐
Using expressions such as *I'll say!* and *I couldn't agree more!* to agree	☐	☐	☐
Understanding expressions such as *You've got to be joking!* and *I guess that's true, but...* when used to disagree	☐	☐	☐
Using expressions such as *You've got to be joking!* and *I guess that's true, but...* to disagree	☐	☐	☐

Think about the topics and activities in this chapter and complete the statements.

In this chapter, I learned something new about _____

_____

_____

I especially liked (topic or activity) _____

_____

_____

I would like to know more about _____

_____

_____

7 Remarkable Individuals

"You gain strength, courage, and confidence by every experience in which you really stop to look fear in the face. You must do the thing you think you cannot do."

Eleanor Roosevelt
First Lady of the U.S. from 1933 to 1945

In this
CHAPTER

Celebrity Profile Lance Armstrong, Uphill Racer

Learning Strategy Listening for Chronological Order

Language Function Expressing Likes and Dislikes,
Pleasure and Displeasure

Connecting to the Topic

1 Who was Eleanor Roosevelt? What remarkable things did she
accomplish?

2 Do you think that mental feats are more or less remarkable than
physical ones? Why?

3 What is the person in the photo doing? Would you be afraid to do
this? Do you think the man's life will be better or worse because
he did this?

Did You Know?

- In 1907, Alphonse Steines was looking for a good location for a bicycle race. While driving in the Pyrenees Mountains in France, he was forced to leave his car in the heavy snow and struggle on foot for 12 km. The next morning, Steines played a joke on his friend Henri Desgrange, the originator of the Tour de France bicycle race, who was also looking for a good location for a race. He telegrammed: "I have crossed the mountains. The roads are passable. No snow." So Henri Desgrange organized the first Tour de France bicycle race in 1910 in the Pyrenees Mountains. The remarkable first racers carried all their own food, clothing, and spare parts with them on their one-speed bikes. Because of Alphonse Steines, Desgrange did not realize that the bikers would also have to pedal through the snow at times and many of the racers did not finish the race.

▲ François Faber, winner of the 1909 Tour de France

- The first American to win the Tour de France bicycle race riding for an American team and on an American bicycle was Lance Armstrong in 1999. The only other American winner, Greg LeMond, was riding for a European team on a European bicycle when he won several times—in 1986, 1989, and 1990. Lance Armstrong won again in 2000, 2001, 2002, 2003, and 2004, breaking the records of four Tour de France riders before him. The previous recordholders, Frenchmen Jacques Anquetil and Bernard Hinault, Belgium's Eddy Merckx, and Spain's Miguel Indurain, had all won five Tours. Armstong went on to surpass his own record with a seventh win in 2005.

1 **What Do You Think?** Take turns speaking about each of the following questions in pairs.

1. What was the joke Alphonse Steines played on Henri Desgrange? What was the result of this joke?

2. Considering the information above, whom do you think is more remarkable: the rider carrying all of his own gear in one of the first Tours de France or Lance Armstrong? Why?

Sharing Your Experience

2 **What Makes an Accomplishment Remarkable?** In this activity you will use a Venn diagram to chart your group's discussion about remarkable feats.

Strategy

Using a Venn Diagram to Show Things That Groups Have In Common
A Venn diagram is a graphic organizer consisting of overlapping circles that shows the relationship between groups. Where two circles overlap, you write what the two groups have in common. Where three circles overlap, you write what all three groups have in common. The rest of each circle can be used to write a group's or person's unique characteristics.

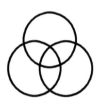

Discuss the following questions in small groups. Copy the Venn diagram below onto poster paper and note the information on your Venn diagram.

1. Who are some of the most remarkable people around the world? What have they done? What do they have in common?

2. Who are some of the most remarkable people you know personally? What have they done? What do they have in common?

3. What do you think is the most remarkable thing you have ever done? Remember: you don't have to be famous to be remarkable. Sometimes the things we accomplish every day are extraordinary.

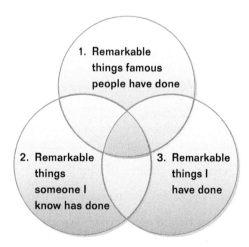

Draw pictures to clarify and enhance your poster. Groups should hang their posters up around the room, then take a "gallery walk" to see what other groups have written.

When everyone has completed the "gallery walk," discuss as a class the similarities and differences that really stand out among the remarkable feats described on the posters.

3 **Sharing Definitions** The definitions of these words correspond to how the words are used in the "celebrity profile" you will hear in this chapter. Work with a partner to write the letter of the correct definition beside each word. Join another pair of students to check your work. Try not to use a dictionary. If your group of four is uncertain about some of the definitions, see if another group can help.

Words

1. _____ battle
2. _____ bull
3. _____ chemotherapy
4. _____ endure
5. _____ fluke
6. _____ from scratch
7. _____ highlight
8. _____ hit-and-run
9. _____ keep up with
10. _____ be riding high
11. _____ undisciplined
12. _____ vertebra

Definitions

a. the most important or best part

b. a fight

c. a section of the spine or backbone

d. to stay equal with

e. a male animal of some species that is strong and aggressive and mates with many females

f. a happy accident; a lucky surprise

g. lacking self-discipline; not following rules

h. from the beginning, starting with nothing

i. to be feeling very happy and confident because of a success

j. involving a car accident in which a driver doesn't stop after hitting someone or something

k. to go through something very difficult and survive

l. a medical treatment for cancer involving the use of drugs

4 **Using Vocabulary** Discuss the following topics and questions with a partner.

1. Describe a personal battle that you have faced. (For example, some students are undisciplined about going to bed and must face the battle of getting out of bed and getting ready for class every morning.) Did you succeed?

2. Describe the qualities of a bull.

3. Have you or has anyone you know ever endured a difficult situation? Describe it.

4. These days it is remarkable to be able to cook anything from scratch. What can you (or your friends or family) make from scratch?

5. What has been the highlight of your successes so far this year? Are you still riding high on it?

6. How many vertebrae do you have? Count them.

FYI

Vertebrae is the plural form of the word *vertebra*.

Strategy

Using Time and Sequence Words as Clues to Chronological Order
Chronological order is a method of organization based on time. Simple chronological order begins with the earliest event and ends with the most recent event. History is often presented in simple chronological order.

Most lectures, however, are more than just a presentation of facts in chronological order. For example, in order to compare recent events with those of the past, a speaker must move forward and backward in time.

Note the following expressions that indicate time or sequence. They will help you follow the actual sequence of events, even if a speaker does not use chronological order.

Time and Sequence Words

- after
- afterward
- at (time)
- at that time
- before
- by (time)
- during
- eventually
- finally
- first
- formerly
- from… to…
- in (month, year)
- in (adjective) times
- last

- later
- long ago
- next
- now
- on (day)
- past
- present
- present day
- presently
- recently
- soon
- then
- today
- until
- while

Strategy

Tuning In to the Logic of Chronological Order

In addition to listening for time and sequence words, it is also important to follow the logic of the facts being presented. Use the following clues to help you understand the time sequence of events, or chronological order.

- Common sense—pay attention to what you know must come first, second, third, etc.
- The use of word repetition to refer to previously mentioned events.
- The use of pronouns to refer to previously mentioned nouns.
- The choice of definite and indefinite articles (*the* versus *a*)—remember: *a* or *an* is used when something has not been mentioned before, and *the* is used when something has already been mentioned once.
- The use of tenses, especially the past perfect tense, which is used to show which of two events in the past happened first.

Before You Listen

1 Putting Events in Chronological Order In small groups, read the three sentences in each "mini-story" aloud. Then use the clues in the strategy above to help you answer the questions about the "mini-stories."

Mini-Story 1

1. By dinnertime he still had not returned.
2. Kristin was waiting for her husband to return from his training ride.
3. Eventually, she phoned his coach to find out what had happened to him.

Which of the sentences should be first? _____

Why? _____

Which should come second? _____

Why? _____

Which is third? _____

Why? _____

Mini-Story 2

1. The other racer was struggling to keep up with him.
2. He was certain now that he would win.
3. While glancing over his left shoulder, Lance saw another racer out of the corner of his eye.

Which of the sentences should be first? _____

Why? _____

Which should come second? _____

Why? _____

Which is third? _____

Why? _____

Mini-Story 3

1. By the end of the three-week race, Voekler had worn the yellow jersey for a remarkable ten days.

2. In 2004, a young rider named Thomas Voekler amazed Tour de France judges and spectators by taking the yellow jersey, symbol of the race leader, away from Armstrong.

3. Even though he knew that his strength was in the "flats" and that Armstrong would eventually overtake him in the mountain stages of the race, he rode on bravely to bring glory to his team and France, his native country and host of the Tour.

Which of the sentences should be first?

_____

▲ Thomas Voekler, trying to hold on to the yellow jersey

Why? _____

Which should come second? _____

Why? _____

Which is third? _____

Why? _____

Listen

2 **Listening for Time and Sequence Expressions** Listen to the celebrity profile once all the way through to get the gist and to accustom yourself to the speaker's vocal mannerisms. Each time you hear one of the time expressions from the Time and Sequence Words list on page 113, make a check mark (✓) beside it.

▲ Lance Armstrong, climbing up a mountain road in the Tour de France

3 **Organizing Information into Chronological Time Periods** Read the statements on the chart below. Then listen to the celebrity profile again. As you listen, put an *X* in the box for the correct time frame for each statement. Listen again, if necessary.

Statements	During Armstrong's youth	Before he found out that he had cancer	After he found out that he had cancer	In the future
1. Armstrong was earning over $1 million a year.				
2. He became an international cycling champion.				
3. He was called the "Bull from Texas."				
4. He met Sheryl Crow.				
5. He built up a lot of heavy muscle.				
6. He built strong and light muscles.				
7. He had a son.				
8. He was hit by a car.				
9. He wants to win a race as his wife and ten children applaud.				
10. He wants to lie in a field of sunflowers.				
11. He was poor.				
12. He won the Tour de France.				

After You Listen

4 **Comparing Your Answers** In small groups, compare your charts. Discuss how you determined the time frame for each item.

5 **Completing a Timeline** With a partner, use your chart and other information you remember from the celebrity profile to fill in key dates and events in the timeline of Lance Armstrong's life on page 117. Add any other events you can think of to the timeline.

Lance Armstrong's Life

He lived in Plano, Texas.	1980s
He was poor.	
	1990
He was called the "Bull from Texas."	1991–1996
	1996
He found out he had cancer.	
He won the Tour de France.	1999
His son Luke was born.	
	2000
He was selected for the U.S. Olympic team.	
	2000
He won a bronze medal.	
	2001
He won the Tour de France.	
	2003
	2004
At the finish line in Paris,	2004

▲ Lance Armstrong with his three children after winning his seventh Tour.

Talk It Over

6 Telling a Story Work in small groups in a circle. Use the following story starters as the first lines of stories. The first student reads the story starter and continues the story by adding another sentence. The second student adds another sentence to the story, the third student adds another one, and so on. Continue in this manner until every student has had at least two turns before you end each story.

As you are making up each story, look back at the list of time and sequence words on page 113 and use as many of them as you can. If possible, record your stories and play them back to the class.

Story Starters

1. Since this was the first day off that Janna had had in over a week, she intended to put her feet up and enjoy a good book. But that isn't what happened! What happened was...

2. Harry hated flying. In fact, you could say that he was a complete coward unless his feet were firmly planted on the ground. But when the plane's engine caught fire...

3. When Sureya was born, she looked quite ordinary. There didn't seem to be anything special about her at all. But when she was about two years old,...

PART 3

Expressing Likes and Dislikes, Pleasure and Displeasure

Strategy

Choosing Appropriate Expressions of Like and Dislike, Pleasure and Displeasure

There are many ways to express likes, dislikes, pleasure, and displeasure. The following expressions are some of the most common and they are listed in order from the gentlest to the strongest.

When choosing an expression of like or dislike, or pleasure or displeasure, the type of situation (whether it's formal or informal, for example) must be considered.

In formal situations, the strongest expressions of dislike and displeasure are probably not appropriate. And even in very informal situations, you might also use one of the gentler expressions of dislike or displeasure when expressing your opinion in order to be considerate of someone's feelings.

In addition, when choosing between making a gentle or a strong statement, you should also consider the following.

- Tone of voice is often more important than the actual expression you choose.
- Anger or sarcasm in your voice cannot be hidden behind the gentlest of expressions.

Expressing Likes/Pleasure		Expressing Dislikes/Displeasure	
gentlest	I like…	**gentlest**	I don't especially/really like…
	I enjoy…		I don't care for…
	I'm pleased…		I dislike…
	I'm happy…		I don't have time for…
	I appreciate…		… bugs me. (informal)
	I'm delighted…		… irks me.
	I'm thrilled…		I can't tolerate…
	This is my idea of…!		… is more than I can stand.
	That's terrific/great/super!		I can't take/stand/bear… !
	What a terrific/great/		What a rotten…!
	super… !		I hate…!
strongest	I love… !	**strongest**	I detest…!

1 Listening for Consequences of Expressions and Tone Listen for the expressions of likes, dislikes, pleasure, and displeasure in the following conversations. Then answer the questions.

Conversation 1

A man is being interviewed for a job.

1. Do you think the man will get the job? _____

2. Why or why not? _____

_____

_____

Conversation 2

A woman is being interviewed for a job.

1. Do you think the woman will get the job? _____

2. Why or why not? _____

_____

_____

Conversation 3

Rafael and Ana are discussing what to do with their leisure time.

1. Does Ana enjoy concerts? _____

2. Does she express her opinion strongly, or does she soften it? _____

3. Do you think Rafael will ask Ana out again? Why or why not? _____

_____

_____

Conversation 4

Rafael and Joyce are discussing what to do with their leisure time.

1. Does Joyce enjoy experimental theater? _____

2. Does she express her opinion strongly? _____

3. Do you think Rafael will ask Joyce out again? Why or why not? _____

_____

_____

2 Listening for Expressions of Likes and Dislikes, Pleasure and Displeasure At several points in the celebrity profile on Lance Armstrong, the speaker expresses a like or a dislike, or pleasure or displeasure. Listen to the profile again. This time, in the chart on page 120, write down all the expressions of like, dislike, pleasure, and displeasure that you hear. When you are finished, compare your answers with those of your classmates.

Expressions used for likes/pleasure	Expressions used for dislikes/displeasure
1.	1.
2.	2.
3.	3.
4.	
5.	

③ Choosing Appropriate Expressions Being polite in a difficult situation is an art. In small groups, decide what to say to the person you meet and to the friend who is with you for each of the following situations. Choose an appropriate expression and tone of voice for expressing likes, dislikes, pleasure, and displeasure. Think about how you would speak with a stranger or acquaintance (formal situation) versus how you would talk to a friend (informal).

Situation 1

A man is sitting in front of you at the movie theater with his three noisy children. They are throwing popcorn at each other and talking too much. You have already asked the father politely to do something about the situation, but there has been no change. It's time to take stronger action. What would you say?

To the father: *I would appreciate it if you could please get your children to quiet down.*

To your friend: *Let's move. I can't stand this.*

Situation 2

You are at a nightclub with your friends. Someone keeps asking you to dance. You think the person is a good dancer, but you are very tired and would prefer just to watch.

To the person: _____

To your friend: _____

Situation 3

Your favorite restaurant is not as good as it used to be. Now the restaurant is not clean, the waiters are rude, and the food is often of poor quality. You and a friend have decided to give the restaurant one last chance, and as you are eating a terrible soup, the owner approaches you and asks you if everything is all right.

To the owner: _____

To your friend: _____

Situation 4

You and a friend have enrolled in a course on public relations and you really love it. The instructor has over 20 years of experience. He has great stories to tell, but most often lectures only on what's in the book. You want to hear more about his "first-hand" experience in public relations.

To the instructor: _____

To your friend: _____

Talk It Over

4 **Discussing Goals and Interests** Look at the following chart of remarkable goals and interests. Circle those things that you would really enjoy doing and draw an *X* through the ones you would not like to do. Add other goals or interests in the blank boxes. In small groups, discuss why you marked your charts the way you did. Use expressions on page 118 to express your likes and dislikes.

Arts	Sports	Home	Career	Relation-ships	Adventure	Other
become an artist	ride a bicycle around the world	build a house from scratch	run a large company	date a movie star	climb Mt. Everest	
take news photos	go bungee jumping	live on a houseboat	win a Nobel Prize	get married more than once	travel to Antarctica	
play in a famous rock band	kick the winning goal at the World Cup soccer finals	have homes in New York, Paris, Tokyo, and Hong Kong	be a fashion model	have a relationship with someone you meet on the Internet	ride in a hot air balloon	
sing at the opera	win an Olympic gold medal in gymnastics	live on a space station	own your own business	make friends with someone from another planet	sail around the world	

F🔍CUS

Questions about Expressing Preference

Some of the questions in the speaking section of the TOEFL® iBT ask if you prefer one thing or another. This type of question would be one of the first two questions in the section.

Example

Some students wash their clothes with machines in on-campus laundry rooms. Others like to take their laundry to laundromats off campus. Which would you prefer, and why? You have 20 seconds to prepare your answer and 45 seconds to speak.

This is a question about likes and dislikes. You like the thing you prefer more than you like the other. You may even dislike the thing you do not prefer.

Some phrases especially useful in expressing preferences are:

- prefer _____ rather than _____
- like _____ more than _____
- would rather _____ than _____

1 **Expressing Preferences** Tell a classmate your preferences in response to the prompts that follow. Use the preference expressions above—and other preference expressions you know—in your responses.

1. Lance Armstrong surely prefers biking to any other sport. Other people prefer less strenuous sports. Which type of sport do you prefer? Why? You have 20 seconds to prepare your answer and 45 seconds to speak.

2. Lance Armstrong would prefer to have many children rather than just one. How about you? Would you prefer to have many children or just one? Why? You have 20 seconds to prepare your answer and 45 seconds to speak.

3. Some people who are injured stop exercising until they are healed. Others, such as Lance Armstrong, quickly resume their activities, even though it might slow their recovery. Which way of dealing with injuries would you prefer? Why? You have 20 seconds to prepare your answer and 45 seconds to speak.

4. Whom do you admire more, a person who becomes famous as an academic (a professor, a researcher, etc.) or a person who succeeds in business? Why? You have 20 seconds to prepare your answer and 45 seconds to speak.

5. Some remarkably talented young people become professional athletes instead of going to college. Others finish their college educations before turning professional. Which would you prefer for yourself if you had remarkable athletic talent? Why? You have 20 seconds to prepare your answer and 45 seconds to speak.

Self-Assessment Log

Check (✓) the words in this chapter you have acquired and can use in your daily life.

Nouns
- battle
- bull
- chemotherapy
- fluke
- highlight
- vertebra

Verbs
- endure
- keep up with

Adjective
- undisciplined

Idioms
- be riding high
- from scratch
- hit-and-run

Check (✓) your level of accomplishment for the skills introduced in this chapter. How comfortable do you feel using these skills?

	Very comfortable	Somewhat comfortable	Not at all comfortable
Listening for chronological order	☐	☐	☐
Organizing information into chronological order	☐	☐	☐
Using expressions such as *I'm delighted...* and *I'm thrilled...* to express likes, pleasure	☐	☐	☐
Determining the appropriateness of expressions such as *I don't care for...* and *I detest...* when used to express dislikes, displeasure	☐	☐	☐
Using expressions such as *I don't care for...* and *I detest...* to express dislikes, displeasure	☐	☐	☐

Think about the topics and activities in this chapter and complete the statements.

In this chapter, I learned something new about _____

_____

_____

I especially liked (topic or activity) _____

_____

_____

I would like to know more about _____

_____

_____

8 Creativity

> Everyone is born creative; everyone is given a box of crayons in kindergarten. Then when you hit puberty they take the crayons away and replace them with books on algebra, etc. Being suddenly hit years later with the creative bug is just a wee voice telling you, 'I'd like my crayons back, please.'

Hugh MacLeod
Cartoonist, author, and corporate CEO

In this
CHAPTER

Lecture Drive and Creativity in the Workplace: The Mismatch Between What Science Knows and What Business Does

Learning Strategy Listening for Signal Words

Language Function Divulging Information

Connecting to the Topic

1. What are the people in the picture trying to accomplish?

2. What might motivate or drive them to do this job?

3. What might drive them to become better at this job?

Did You Know?

- In 1996, Microsoft launched MSN Encarta, a multimillion dollar online encyclopedia and paid millions to professional writers and editors to create articles on thousands of topics. However, in 2009, Microsoft abandoned this product because it could not compete with Wikipedia.

- According to Daniel H. Pink, a contributor to *The New York Times* and *Harvard Business Review*, Wikipedia represents the most powerful new business model of the twenty-first century: open-source, which is where volunteer contributors create the product. The open-source model, which virtually has no paid employees, has also been used to create Firefox, a highly popular web browser, Linux, a program that now powers one in four corporate computer servers, and Apache, whose website software is used by 52% of the web-server market.

- Nobel Peace Prize winner Muhammad Yunus has begun creating "social businesses" that raise money, develop products, and sell them in an open or free market just as traditional businesses do. However, these "social businesses" are "not only for profit" and they focus on social benefits as well as profit maximization. Mozilla, the company that created Firefox, is an example of a "for-benefit" organization.

▲ Author Daniel Pink

▲ Nobel Peace Prize winner Muhammad Yunus

1 What Do You Think? In pairs, take turns speaking about each of the following questions.

1. What do you think are the qualities that MSN Encarta and Wikipedia might have in common? What are the qualities that might be very different? Why do you think Wikipedia beat MSN Encarta in the marketplace?

2. What do you think might be some other businesses or projects that use an open-source model? What might be the pros and cons of the open-source model?

3. What do you think are some ways that "social businesses" might be improving the quality of their products as well as maximizing their profits?

2 **What Motivates You at Work, at School, and at Play** Think about the activities you are involved in. What motivates you or drives you to do well at these activities? Fill in the chart below with specific activities that you do at work, at school, and at play and what drives you to do them well. Then share your responses in small groups.

What Drives You...?		
At Work	At School	At Play

3 **When and Where Have You Been the Most Creative** Think about the times and places in which you have been the most creative. Jot down a few notes about what helped you to be so creative in each situation. Then share your thoughts in small groups.

The Situation: Time and Place	What helped you to be so creative in this situation?

4 **How to Be More Creative** Wiki-How, an offshoot of Wikipedia, lists the following ways to become more creative. In small groups, discuss what you think each statement means and why you agree or disagree with it.

Ways to Become More Creative		
Ways	Meaning	Agree or Disagree? Why?
1. Limit your selection of tools for a task to the most important ones.		
2. Don't listen to feedback. Just keep following your own path.		
3. Stick to a routine.		
4. Let go of perfectionism.		
5. Ignore trends.		
6. Ignore the past.		

5 **Vocabulary in Context** These words are used in the lecture on drive and creativity. Complete the following sentences with the correct forms of the vocabulary words.

Words	Definitions
addictive	*so enjoyable that you want to do it all the time*
crush	*to press down or suppress; to completely overcome*
ethics	*moral principles or values*
flaw	*something very wrong; a mistake or fault*
greedy	*wanting much more than you need*
inhibit	*to slow down or hold back*
maximization	*taking full advantage of or getting the most out of something*
mortgage broker	*a person who finds loans for those wishing to buy property*
recession	*a period during which there is a decline in economic trade and prosperity*
recruit	*to look for and then hire workers*
shortcut	*a route that is shorter or more direct than the usual one*
tap into	*to make use of a resource or supply of something*
unethical	*not behaving morally or following the agreed-upon standards*

1. Earning millions of dollars a year became so _____ that when the _____ hit and Bob's salary was reduced by the company, he was tempted to do some very immoral things to get more money.

2. Being _____ was not Mary's only _____. She was also _____. She seemed to want not just one, but two of everything.

▲ Is this man greedy?

3. The company decided that _____ of profits was so important that they were willing to ignore established _____ in the field and take a _____ around the laws.

4. In order to _____ the best workers, companies must create an environment that does not _____ or even _____ creativity.

5. A competent _____ will _____ all possible sources to find a home buyer the best loan.

Strategy

Listening for Signal Words to Guide Note-Taking

When speaking, we often use signal words to prepare our audience for what is to come, for what our next idea will be. This allows the audience to listen more effectively. Listening for signal words is especially important when attending a lecture because it helps us take notes. If an instructor says, "Now I'm going to outline today's subject for you," we know to prepare ourselves to do outlining. If the instructor says, "Now I'm going to review yesterday's material," we know to think about the topic covered the day before and to look back over those notes. Signal words prepare us for what is going to happen and what we need to do in response.

Some Verbs that Serve as Signal Words

analyze	emphasize	list
answer	evaluate	outline
consider	explain	pick up (where we left off)
continue	give an example	repeat
define	go on (with)	review
describe	go over	summarize
discuss	illustrate	take up

Before You Listen

1 **Considering the Topic** Think about the following questions. Then, in small groups, share your thoughts about each question.

1. What are the rewards that companies can provide workers besides money?
2. Should workers be punished if they do not produce? If not, why? If yes, how?
3. Why is creativity so important in today's economy?
4. What might inhibit creativity in the workplace?
5. What are some ways that companies might increase creativity in the workplace?

Listen

2 **Listening for Main Points About Drive and Creativity** Listen to
the lecture once all the way through (Parts 1 and 2) to familiarize yourself with the
speaker's style and tone.

Listen again to Part 1 of the lecture in which the lecturer gives some background
information on the topic. Fill in the blanks in the following sentences as you listen.

1. Pink says that it is the misunderstanding of what actually _____
   us that inhibits creativity and productivity in the workplace.

2. Traditionally in the workplace, management has motivated people to work
   harder, faster—better—with a system of _____ that we
   commonly call _____.

3. First, because carrots and sticks are _____ motivators, they can
   extinguish _____ motivators.

4. The second deadly flaw is that carrots and sticks can actually
   _____ performance rather than _____ it.

5. The third deadly flaw is that carrots and sticks can _____
   creativity.

6. The fourth deadly flaw of the carrot and stick model is that it can crowd out
   _____ behavior.

7. The fifth deadly flaw is that carrots and sticks can encourage
   _____, _____, and _____
   behavior.

8. The sixth flaw is that rewards can become _____ and people
   may take great risks to gain these rewards.

9. The seventh and worst flaw of the carrot and stick model according to Pink is
   that it encourages _____ rather than _____.

What might motivate these people to be more creative at work?

Listen again to Part 2 of the lecture. As you listen, list and define what Pink says are the three essential elements for promoting drive and creativity in the workplace.

1. _____

_____

_____

_____

_____

2. _____

_____

_____

_____

_____

3. _____

_____

_____

_____

_____

 3 **Listening for Signal Words** Listen to the lecture again. This time, listen for the signal words in the box on page 130. Every time you hear one of these words or phrases, put a check mark (✓) next to it. Listen until you have heard at least eight signal words.

Listen to the lecture again. This time, pay particular attention to what happens *after* each signal word or phrase.

- Write the signal word or phrase in the left column of the following chart.
- In the right column of the chart, note what the speaker does after each signal word. (**Hint:** If the lecturer has used the signal word effectively, your answer will include a definition or synonym for this word.) Underline the synonym once.
- Note the topic or content the lecturer covers after each signal word. You may need to listen to the lecture again.

Signal words	What comes next: what the lecturer does plus what topic/content the lecturer covers
1. continue	<u>goes on with</u> the discussion of the creative process by taking up the topic of what things might inhibit creativity in the workplace
2. take up	continue with the discussion of the creative process by starting with the topic of what things might inhibit creativity in the workplace

4 **Comparing Notes** With a partner, compare your notes from Activities 2 and 3.

1. Did you fill in the blanks with the same words? If not, how did they differ?
2. Did you list and describe the same three essential elements to promote drive and creativity? If not, how did they differ?
3. Did you check off the same signal words? If not, how were they different?
4. Did you agree on what the speaker did and said after each signal word? If not, how did you disagree?

Talk It Over

5 **Using Your Creativity to Solve Puzzles** In the lecture on drive and creativity in the workplace, the lecturer describes a study in which university students were given a series of puzzles to solve that required concentration and creativity. Try to use your creativity to solve the following puzzles. Then share your creative solutions with the class.

1. Look at the "Dot Puzzle" below. Connect the nine dots in the box by drawing no more than four straight connected lines.
2. Devised by psychologist Karl Duncker, the "Candle Problem" below is used in a wide variety of experiments in behavioral science. Imagine you are sitting a table next to a wooden wall and you are given the materials shown: a candle, some tacks, and a book of matches. Your job is to fix the candle to the wall so that the wax from the candle doesn't drip on the table.

▲ Dot Puzzle

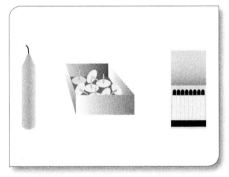

▲ Candle Problem

6 **Using Your Creativity to Brainstorm Solutions**
Imagine you are in a situation with another person in which you are not allowed to speak or write. The exact situation is not important, but if it helps, you might imagine that you are:

- walking on Mars with a fellow astronaut, you find that your radio system between space suits is broken
- sitting across the room from each other in a courtroom
- sitting across the room from each other during a speech or ceremony

In small groups, brainstorm what methods you could devise to communicate with the other person.

- Put your responses on poster paper.
- Add pictures to elaborate.
- Share your posters with the class and act out the various methods, making sure each group member has a chance to participate.

Strategy

Recognizing Tone of Voice and Body Language Signals
Human beings use more than language to signal each other. Two signals that people use, often unconsciously, are tone of voice and body language. Tone of voice and body language can tell us how people really feel despite their actual words. As people's moods and intentions change, their voices and bodies reflect those changes. If you are alert, you can read the deeper, or perhaps truer, meanings of the words people say by noticing the tone they use and their posture, gestures, and other body language.

7 Using Tone of Voice and Body Language Signals To get a feeling for the power of tone of voice and body language as you communicate, push back the desks and stand in a circle with your classmates and instructor.

- Take turns saying an insignificant sentence to someone across the room from you. Take a few steps as you say the sentence to get your whole body into the act, not just your face and voice. Use this sentence (or make up your own if you prefer):

    Apples are red and bananas are yellow.

- Next, take turns saying the sentence "with a particular attitude." Your instructor or a classmate will call out an adjective to describe the attitude you should have as you say the sentence. Here are a few adjectives to get you started. Add as many as you can to this list.

| angry | disgusted | frightened | grieving | inhibited | murderous | sarcastic |
| delighted | flirtatious | frustrated | hopeful | joyful | rushed | shy |

_____

_____

_____

_____

_____

_____

FYI

We have been discussing a couple of ways that signaling occurs in language. But other kinds of signaling go on all the time among human beings, animals, insects, plants, and even individual cells. For example, cells send chemical messages to one another; plants use pollen, scent, and insects to send messages; birds use markings, like the color of their feathers, and sound.

8 Researching the Topic We have been discussing some ways that signaling occurs in language. But other kinds of signaling go on all the time among human beings, animals, insects, plants, and even individual cells. For example, cells send chemical messages to one another; plants use pollen, scent, and insects to send messages; birds use markings, such as the color of their feathers, and sound.

Below are the names of some animals and insects that are well known for their ability to signal and communicate. Form small discussion groups. Each person should choose one of the animals or insects listed (or any other you know about).

whales	ants	chimpanzees	mockingbirds	skunks
bees	dogs	dolphins	cockroaches	gorillas

1. Research to find out how the animal or insect signals and communicates. Make notes to use for a brief talk on this topic. If you search on the Internet for information, try these keywords: (*the name of the animal/insect*), *language, communication, sign language, signals.*

2. Meet with your group again. Take turns describing the major ways each animal or insect communicates. Use signal words in your talk to prepare your classmates for what will come next.

▲ A chimpanzee uses sign language to tell her trainer that she wants to hug the cat.

3. Discuss these questions after everyone in your group has had a chance to present.

- How do these animal or insect forms of communication compare to human communication?
- Are the animals or insects as creative? Do they just do the same thing over and over or do they see things in new ways and develop new signs and signals to communicate what they experience?

PART 3 Divulging Information

Strategy

Recognizing When Information is Being Divulged

To divulge means "to give out or disclose." If someone is divulging information, the implication is that he or she is telling something important that most people may not know, "the inside information," "what is really happening," or "the *real* story."

Information that is *divulged* is of a different quality than other information given during a conversation or a lecture. It is important in note-taking and outlining that you recognize when information is being divulged because it could very likely be that the instructor wants you to take this information seriously and that means that it could very well be on the next test.

When a lecturer is about to divulge something, he or she usually announces this intention by using one of the following expressions.

Expressions for Divulging Information
Despite what you may believe...
Despite what you may have heard...
Here's how it really is.
In fact...
The fact of the matter is...
The reality is...
The truth is...
What's really going on here is...

Informal Expressions for Divulging Information
Here's the real story.
The real deal is...
The real scoop is...
The (real) story is...
What's really going on is...

1 Listening for Ways of Divulging Information Listen to these conversations that present examples of ways to divulge information.

Conversation 1

Antoine and Dashika are discussing the real reason that their colleague left their company.

Listen to the speakers and answer the questions.

1. Is this conversation formal or informal? _____

2. What phrase helped you decide this? _____

Conversation 2

Katya and David are discussing where Jesse got the cash for his new motorcycle.

Listen to the speakers and answer the questions.

1. Is this conversation formal or informal?_____

2. What phrase helped you decide this? _____

2 Listening for Information That Is Divulged Listen to the lecture again. Write down the phrases that signal that information is about to be divulged. Listen also for the specific information that is divulged and record it on the chart as well. Discuss with your classmates whether or not the information that the lecturer divulges is critical to the main points of the lecture.

Phrases the lecturer uses to divulge information	Information divulged
1.	
2.	
3.	
4.	
5.	

Talk It Over

3 Completing Conversations Look at the following incomplete conversations. With a partner, complete as many of the conversations as you can in the time you are given. Use as many of the expressions for divulging information on page 137 as you can. Choose one conversation and role-play it for the class.

Conversation 1

A: What's up? I hear Frank's leaving the university.

B: Nah, _____

A: _____

B: _____

Conversation 2

A: I don't understand why Shin has been so excited lately. Helen tells me one thing and Jean tells me another. What's going on?

B: _____

A: _____

B: _____

Conversation 3

A: I just saw Professor McNab, and he said the test was cancelled. I thought that he never cancelled tests, no matter what. What's the story?

B: _____

A: _____

B: _____

Conversation 4

A: Hey, what gives? I thought you'd gotten an A in that class. Paul says that you impressed everyone with your last creative writing project.

B: _____

A: _____

B: _____

Conversation 5

A: Where do you think I should exhibit my paintings? Henry suggested the gallery over by the museum, but Vicki said that not many people go there.

B: _____

A: _____

B: _____

Conversation 6

A: Hey, I thought this was supposed to be an open book test! And why is the TA here and not the professor? What's the scoop?

B: _____

A: _____

B: _____

FOCUS

Signal Words and Divulging Information

Throughout this book, you have been learning how important it is to take notes during lectures and in particular to take notes efficiently on the TOEFL® iBT. In Part 2 of this chapter, you learned about *signal words* and how recognizing these words will help you to take notes on important information. In Part 3 of this chapter, you learned about *divulging information* and how listening for expressions used for this purpose can also help you to note information that a lecturer may think is important.

1 **Note-Taking Practice** Close your books and listen to the conversation that follows between a student and an instructor. Pay particular attention to the signal words and other expressions that you've learned about in Chapters 1–8 that a speaker may use to call attention to important information. Take notes. Then open your books and answer the questions.

1. What was the student confused about? (choose two)
   - (A) something that was said in class
   - (B) something about the arts being necessary for creativity
   - (C) something about training being necessary for creativity
   - (D) something about training not being necessary for creativity

2. Why does the professor use Jean-Michel Basquiat as an illustration?
   - (A) because he is dead
   - (B) because he never had any formal training as a painter
   - (C) because he is famous
   - (D) because his paintings are in museums

3. Listen to part of the conversation again.

   Why does the professor say, "and I can't emphasize this enough"?
   - (A) because she doesn't know any other examples
   - (B) because she already explained this yesterday
   - (C) because she thinks what she is about to say is a very important point
   - (D) because Basquiat is famous

4. What does the professor imply about van Gogh's work? (choose two)
   - (A) It was ahead of its time.
   - (B) It was only creative while van Gogh was alive.
   - (C) We should measure the worth of a painting by how much it costs.
   - (D) Even though these days people generally appreciate van Gogh's work, many people of his generation did not.

5. Listen to part of the conversation again.

Why does the student say, "This may sound a little naïve, but…"?

(A) because he is very young

(B) because he is innocent

(C) because he is afraid his idea may sound overly simple, incorrect, or incomplete

(D) because he is sure his question is a stupid one

Self-Assessment Log

Check (✓) the words in this chapter you have acquired and can use in your daily life.

Nouns
- ethics
- flaw
- maximization
- mortgage broker
- recession
- shortcut

Verbs
- crush
- inhibit
- recruit
- tap into

Adjectives
- addictive
- greedy
- unethical

Check (✓) your level of accomplishment for the skills introduced in this chapter. How comfortable do you feel using these skills?

	Very comfortable	Somewhat comfortable	Not at all comfortable
Listening for signal words to take better notes	☐	☐	☐
Understanding expressions such as *Despite what you may have heard…* and *The real story is…* when used to divulge information	☐	☐	☐
Using expressions such as *Despite what you may have heard* and *The real story is…* to divulge information	☐	☐	☐

Think about the topics and activities in this chapter and complete the statements.

In this chapter, I learned something new about _____

_____

_____

I especially liked (topic or activity) _____

_____

_____

I would like to know more about _____

_____

_____

9 Human Behavior

Americans of all
ages, all stations in
life, and all types
of disposition are
forever constantly
forming associations.

Alexis de Tocqueville
French author and statesman

In this CHAPTER

Lecture Group Dynamics

Learning Strategy Recognizing Digressions

Language Function Using Tag Questions to Ask for Information or Confirmation, or to Challenge

 Connecting to the Topic

1. Where do you guess these people are and what do you think they are watching?

2. Do you think most people would attend this activity alone? Why or why not?

3. Would you rather be watching or participating in this activity? Why?

Did You Know?

- Associations exist for just about every interest you can imagine. For example, the International Laughter Society's members promote laughter as a remedy for illness and as an aid to increase productivity at work; presumably, the people in the Young American Bowling Alliance enjoy bowling tournaments for young people; and an association called the Giraffe Project has members who "stick their necks out" to help other people in ways that involve physical, financial, or social risk.

▲ Volunteer members of Habitat for Humanity enjoy working together to build a home for a deserving family.

- Between 86% and 90% of Americans belong to an organized group or club. Seven out of ten Americans belong to at least one organization that is devoted to helping others or improving the community. Members of a group called Habitat for Humanity, including former U.S. President Jimmy Carter, choose to swing a hammer rather than a golf club on a weekend off in order to build houses for people who cannot afford to buy them in the usual way.

1 What Do You Think? With a partner, take turns speaking about each of the following.

1. What are some of the reasons that people volunteer to work with a group such as Habitat for Humanity?

2. Every time a project is completed, one lucky family receives a house, but what do the volunteers get? (**Hint:** Think about feelings and not things.)

2 **How Sociable Are You?** Where would you rather be right now? With a group? Or doing something on your own? Think about where you were, what you did, and who you were with one day last week and complete the chart before breaking into small groups.

Time	Alone or with other people?	Number of people you were with	Activity
8:00 A.M.			
10:00 A.M.			
12:00 noon			
2:00 P.M.			
4:00 P.M.			
6:00 P.M.			
8:00 P.M.			
10:00 P.M.			
12:00 midnight			

In small groups, share the following information from your chart.

1. How many hours were you alone?
2. How many hours were you with others?
3. What activity took up most of your time?
4. What types of group activities did you participate in? Sports? Work? Social events? Clubs? Family activities? Other?
5. Was this a typical day for you and the people you were with? Why or why not?

Discuss the following questions with the whole class.

1. Are people in the class similar or different in the amount of time they spend alone and with other people?
2. Would you prefer to spend more time, less time, or the same amount of time with other people? Why?

3 Vocabulary in Context The underlined words and phrases in the passages below are used in the lecture on group dynamics that you will hear in this chapter. Read the three possible definitions for each underlined word or phrase. Then choose the definition that best fits the word or phrase as it is used in the sentence.

Example

Many international students already have chosen a particular field of interest before they arrive at school. For example, some want to study science, others want to study art, and others want to study literature.

(A) a piece of land with no trees

(B) a division of academic study

(C) a place where oil is found

1. Joe feels his position as president of a political group on campus is an important part of his identity and he cannot imagine giving up this job. Who would he be if he weren't president?

(A) individuality, the condition of being oneself

(B) intellect, intelligence

(C) innocence, lack of experience

2. A number of random, unrelated events contributed to Joe's joining the group.

(A) chance

(B) well-planned

(C) cheap

3. Joe can pretty much do whatever he wants because he has plenty of money; that's why he can volunteer so many hours for the group's project.

(A) never

(B) hardly ever

(C) mostly

4. Joe has good communication skills and is aware that in some cultures, eye contact is important when speaking to someone.

(A) looking directly into someone's eyes

(B) agreeing with someone

(C) knowing someone's eye color

5. When Joe's friend Yoshiko is concentrating hard on what Joe is telling the group, she winds her hair around her finger over and over.

(A) blows

(B) plants

(C) wraps

6. Joe took five minutes at the end of a group meeting to <u>recap</u> his ideas just in case we had forgotten what he had said.

- (A) change
- (B) bottle
- (C) summarize

Strategy

Recognizing Digressions and Returns to the Main Topic
Most lecturers *digress* from time to time. That is, they go off the topic. Digressions are usually used to offer something extra. Information in digressions is not generally included on exams.

Lecturers digress for a number of reasons:

- A lecturer might have an interesting or amusing idea or story that does not relate directly to the subject.

- A lecturer may want to connect a new idea to something the students already know.

- A lecturer may want to help students become more involved in a particular topic. In this case, the lecturer might suggest activities or readings students can do on their own.

- A lecturer might see the students getting tired and want to give them a chance to relax for a few minutes.

When lecturers digress too much, however, it can be difficult to follow the lecture. Therefore:

- Most lecturers are careful to point out to students when they are beginning a digression. Sometimes a lecturer begins a digression by announcing it with an apology or request for permission.

- Similarly, when completing a discussion, lecturers will often use special expressions to indicate to students that they are returning to the main topic.

Expressions for Announcing Digressions

(Just) As an aside...	Oh, I forgot to mention...
By the way...	Oh, that makes me think of...
If I may digress...	Oh, that reminds me...
If I may stray from the subject...	Oh, yes...
If I may wander...	To change the subject...
If you'll let me digress for a moment...	To go/get off on a tangent for a moment...
Let me digress...	To go/get off the topic for a moment...
Let me just mention that...	To wander for just a moment...
Let me mention in passing that...	

Expressions for Announcing a Return to the Main Topic

Anyway...	To get back to the topic at hand...
Anyway, as I was saying...	To go on with what I was saying...
As I started to say...	To return to what I was saying...
Back to our main topic...	Well, back to business...
(But) Enough of...	Well, back to work...
To come back to what I was saying...	Well, to continue (with the main topic)...
To continue with our main point...	

Before You Listen

1 Considering the Topic Discuss the following questions in small groups. Make your best guesses based on your own experience and observations.

1. In a group of six people in a social situation, do you think everyone talks an equal amount? If not, how many people do you think do most of the talking?

2. When eating dinner with a group of friends, whom do you think people talk to most? The person next to them? The person across from them? The host at the head of the table?

3. Do you think most people work better in groups or alone? Why?

4. Do you think most people work better with or without an audience? Why?

5. Whom do you think is best-liked in a social group? The person who talks the most? The person who talks the least? Or the person who talks a moderate amount?

2 Discussing Digressions Informal conversations among friends or family are often one digression after another. In small groups, discuss the following questions about digressions.

▲ Digressions are sometimes the most fun parts of informal conversations.

1. What are some specific reasons people might use digressions in informal conversations?

2. When do you think digressions are most useful?

3. When might a digression be impolite? Are there any circumstances in which it would be impolite *not* to digress?

3 **Making an Educated Guess about Digressions** With a partner, read the following statements (items 1–12) from the lecture. Make an "educated guess," a guess based on what you already know, about which statements relate to the main points in the lecture and which statements are digressions. Then write your guess in the column for "Main point or digression." You will fill in information in the other two columns in Activity 4.

Statement	Main point or digression	Phrase used to introduce the digression	Reason for the digression
1. "This afternoon I'm going to talk about a topic that affects every person in this room—group dynamics."	*main point*		
2. "First, we'll look at patterns of communication in groups, and then we'll look at how groups affect individual performance."			
3. "You all went to the discussion session yesterday, didn't you?"			
4. "It doesn't seem to matter how large the group is—only a few people talk at once."			

Statement	Main point or digression	Phrase used to introduce the digression	Reason for the digression
5. "I must tell you that all the research I know about has been done in the United States and Canada."			
6. "The research shows that in groups of eight or more, people talk to the people sitting across the table from them."			
7. "If you're planning to be a matchmaker and start a romance between two of your friends, don't seat them next to each other at your next dinner party."			
8. "The theory behind this type of research—research that demonstrates that people do better work in groups—is called social facilitation theory."			
9. "In this way, we're like a number of other creatures."			
10. "As I mentioned earlier, there is also research that demonstrates the opposite— that individuals perform worse, not better, on tasks when other people are there."			
11. "If you don't already know how to do something, you will probably make some mistakes. And if you have an audience, you will continue to make mistakes."			
12. "If you can manage it, you should take tests on a stage in front of a large audience."			
How many items did you guess were digressions?			

4 Listening for Digressions Listen to the lecture. Listen once all the way through to get the gist, or general idea, of the topic, and to adjust to the speaker's voice. Then listen again.

- Listen again. As you listen, check your guesses about the statements in Activity 3 by noting the phrases the lecturer uses to introduce digressions. Write them in the chart beside the digressions they introduce.
- Then note the reasons for the digressions. Use the following abbreviations to save time:

AI = to keep the audience interested
C = to connect abstract ideas to real experiences
PAI = to provide additional information
R = to relax the audience

5 **Listening for Returns to the Main Topic** Look over the expressions used to announce a return to the main topic once more. Then listen to the lecture again. As you listen, note which expressions the lecturer uses to return to the main topic by putting a check (✓) next to an expression in the box on page 148 each time you hear it.

6 **Listening for Specific Information** Write down what the lecturer says about the following questions.

1. In a social group, does everyone talk more or less the same amount or differing amounts? _____

_____

2. At a dinner party, whom do people talk with the most? _____

_____

3. Do people work better in groups or alone? _____

Why? _____

_____

_____

4. Do most people work better with or without an audience? _____

Why? _____

_____

_____

5. Who is best-liked in a social

group? _____

_____

Why? _____

_____

_____

_____

_____

▲ Will this young man play better with or without an audience?

7 **Comparing Answers** Compare your answers from Activities 4, 5, and 6, with your classmates. Answer the following questions as you discuss Activities 4 and 5.

1. How many digressions did each person hear? _____

2. Which expressions were used to introduce the digressions? _____

3. What was the most frequent reason for a digression? _____

4. What was the least frequent reason? _____

5. Which expressions were used to return to the main topic? _____

When you compare your answers from Activity 6 with your classmates, look at your "best guesses" from Activity 1 when you considered the topic of group dynamics. Did anyone guess everything that the lecturer would say on this subject?

Talk It Over

8 **Reporting on Digressions** Sit in on a class or attend a public lecture or meeting of a club that interests you. The newspaper probably lists the time and place of events that are open to the public. If you can't attend a lecture or meeting, listen to one on television or the radio.

1. Listen for the digressions in the lecture. When you hear a digression, make a note of what it is about, of the phrase used to introduce it, and the reason the lecturer used it. Use the same abbreviations that you used in Activity 4 to save time (AI, C, PAI, and R).

2. Report your findings to your class and compare notes using the chart below.

How many digressions did each person hear?	
What is the average number of digressions class members heard per lecture?	
What was the most frequent reason for a digression?	
What was the least frequent reason?	

9 **Discussing Group Activities** In small groups, look at the list of activities below. Add other activities to the list if you wish. Choose three topics and discuss how any of the principles of group dynamics presented in the lecture might apply to the activities you chose.

dating	going to see a band	_____
going to the movies	investing money as a group	_____
playing a team sport	going dancing at a nightclub	_____
studying in a group	working on a team project	_____
eating out	sharing a room or apartment	_____

▲ How might the principles of group dynamics affect this group of students at a friend's birthday party?

1. Write down the topics your group has chosen.

   Topic 1 _____

   Topic 2 _____

   Topic 3 _____

2. Discuss the topics one at a time. During the discussions, members of the group should try to get off the topic by digressing. Be sure to use expressions to introduce your digressions.

3. If you are successful and get the group to listen to your digression, practice using appropriate expressions to return to the main point.

Strategy

**Understanding and Using the Three Types of Tag Questions:
Genuine, Rhetorical, and Challenging**

Tag questions are questions added or "tagged on" at the end of a statement. They are very short, usually consisting of only a subject and an auxiliary verb. (See list of exceptions below.) However, tag questions are used frequently, so it is important for you to have a good grasp of the three types of tag questions, their different purposes and how intonation plays a big part in conveying the intention or purpose of each tag question. It is also critical to sort out when tag questions can be affirmative and when they can be negative.

1. Genuine Tag Questions (asking for information)

Genuine tag questions are used to ask for information. Here the speaker sincerely wants to know the answer. The genuine tag question has rising intonation.

Example You're coming to soccer practice today, aren't you?

Genuine tag questions can be either affirmative or negative. If the statement is affirmative, the tag question is always negative. If the statement is negative, the tag question is always affirmative.

Example You're not coming to soccer practice today, are you?

2. Rhetorical Tag Questions (asking for agreement or confirmation)

A rhetorical tag question indicates that the speaker knows the answer already and just wants confirmation or agreement from the listener. The rhetorical question has falling intonation.

Example You've come to every game, haven't you?

Rhetorical tag questions can be either affirmative or negative. As with genuine tag questions, if the statement is affirmative, the tag question is negative. If the statement is negative, the tag question is affirmative.

Example You've not come to every game, have you?

3. Challenging Tag Questions (to challenge an attitude or action)

When using a challenging tag question, the speaker uses an affirmative statement followed by an affirmative tag question to signal a challenge, indicating: "You're (he's, she's, they're) not going to get away with that." The challenging tag question has rising intonation, but it rises more suddenly than the genuine question does.

Example So they think they're going to win the match, do they?

Expressions Used as Tag Questions

The following expressions are used as tag questions and do not necessarily follow the pattern of other tag questions containing a subject and auxiliary verb.

Expression	Example
OK?	You'll be the goalie today, OK?
Right?	The score is 2-2, right?
Huh?	So you thought we'd lose, huh?
Don't you think?	He plays a fine game of tennis, don't you think?
Don't you agree?	Derek Jeter is a great athlete, don't you agree?

1 **Conveying Intention of Tag Questions with Intonation** With a partner, take turns practicing tag questions in the box on page 156 in three ways.

1. First, say the tag questions as genuine questions with rising intonation to ask for information. Discuss a possible situation in which the statement and tag question might actually be used.

   Example of a genuine question
   You're going to be there tomorrow, aren't you?

   Situation
   The speaker doesn't know whether the listener will actually be coming tomorrow or not.

2. Then change each of the tag questions to a rhetorical question with falling intonation to get confirmation or agreement. Again discuss a situation in which the statement and tag question might be used.

   Example of a rhetorical question
   You're going to be there tomorrow, aren't you?

   Situation
   The speaker already knows that the listener will be coming tomorrow and just wants confirmation of this.

3. Finally, change each of the tag questions to a challenging question with sharply rising intonation (and an overall tone of irritation in your voice). You will also have to change any negative statements or tag questions to positive ones. Again, suggest a possible scenario for each of these challenging questions.

   Example of a genuine question (rising intonation) or rhetorical question (falling intonation)
   So they don't think they're going to win the match, do they?

   Changed to a challenging question
   So they think they're going to win the match, do they?

   Situation
   Perhaps this person is tired of the other team winning all the time and constantly bragging about it.

Statements to Say in Three Ways

1. You're coming to soccer practice today, aren't you?
2. You've come to every game, haven't you?
3. We're not going to play today, are we?
4. So they've won ten more games than we have, haven't they?
5. She's not going to quit the team, is she?
6. They don't want to hire any new coaches this year, do they?
7. She thinks he's the cutest player on the team, doesn't she?

 2 Listening for Intonation Patterns Listen to the following conversations that include tag questions. Answer the questions after each conversation.

▲ "So he thinks he's going to score another goal, does he?" Genuine, rhetorical, or challenging?

Conversation 1

Steven is telling Tom about the first soccer practice of the season, which is only two days away.

What intonation pattern does Steven use—genuine question, rhetorical question, or challenging question?

_____

_____

Conversation 2

All week, Steven and Tom have been looking forward to playing soccer on Saturday. Steven is telling a third friend, George, about the practice.

What intonation pattern does Steven use this time—genuine question, rhetorical question, or challenging question?

_____

_____

Conversation 3

Soccer practice has been arranged for 6:30 A.M. because another team has reserved the field for 8:30. Tom and Steven are talking about Karl, who told Tom that he wouldn't be coming until 8:00.

What intonation pattern does Steven use here—genuine question, rhetorical

question, or challenging question? _____

Conversation 4

Charlie's boss expects a report on Friday but realizes that it would be useful at a meeting on Wednesday.

What intonation pattern does the boss use—genuine question, rhetorical

question, or challenging question? _____

Conversation 5

Josie comes home and sees Peter, one of her housemates, sitting in the living room with his feet up. Since it's already 6:00, she concludes that it's not his turn to cook.

1. What single-word tag questions are used in this conversation? _____

_____

_____

2. Are they used as genuine questions, rhetorical questions, or challenging

questions? _____

_____

 3 **Listening for the Three Types of Tag Questions** Listen to the lecture again. This time, notice the tag questions. As you listen, complete the following chart. Write sentences with positive "tags" in the "Affirmative" row, negative "tags" in the "Negative" row, and sentences with other words or phrases functioning as tag questions in the "Other" row. Write the sentences in the appropriate column depending on whether it is genuine, rhetorical, or challenging. When you are finished, compare your chart with those of your classmates. If there are differences, listen to the lecture again and see if you can agree this time.

	Genuine	Rhetorical	Challenging
Affirmative			
Negative		*I'm sure that you belong to other groups, too, don't you?*	
Other			

 4 **Using Tag Questions to Ask for and Confirm Information** In medium-sized groups of five to eight, get confirmation from one person at a time about his or her leisure activities.

- Use only statements followed by tag questions.
- If you are not sure what this person does during his or her leisure time, make a guess followed by a genuine tag question (with rising intonation).
- If you definitely know one of this person's leisure activities, make a statement followed by a rhetorical tag question (with falling intonation).
- When this person has answered all the tag questions from the group, use tag questions to get confirmation from another member of the group.

Examples

You like to play handball, don't you?   or   You don't like to play handball, do you?

You're a terrific dancer, aren't you?   or   You don't like to dance, do you?

Your collection of jazz is huge, isn't it?   or   You don't collect jazz, do you?

5 **Using Tag Questions in Role-Plays** In groups of four, role-play a few of the following situations or create some of your own.

- Use as many tag questions—and *types* of tag questions—as you can. Then present your role-plays to the class.
- Keep score of the number of genuine, rhetorical, and challenging tag questions each group uses. You might give bonus points for using challenging tags in the role-plays because these can be quite tricky to use appropriately.
- Total the scores for each group.
- Which group used the most tag questions? _____
- Which group used the most types of tag questions? _____
- Which group used the most challenging tag questions? _____

Situations

1. During a break between sets at a music concert, half of a group of friends decides the band is awful and wants to leave; the other half thinks it's great and wants to stay.

▲ "This band is great, don't you think?"

2. At a restaurant, friends are deciding whether to split the bill equally, have each person pay exactly her or his share, or let one person have a turn paying the whole thing.

"It's my turn to pay, isn't it?" ▶

3. You and some friends are on a mountain camping trip. Although you had planned to stay for five days, it's starting to snow on the second day. Discuss what you should do.

4. At the office, the boss has suggested a ten-hour day with a four-day work week. The employees are told that they will be able to make the final decision as a group, but while some of them like to have long weekends, others prefer to spread out their leisure time over the entire week.

5. At home one evening, you receive a phone call saying that you've just won an all-expenses-paid vacation to Hawaii. You may bring one friend. Your best friends are sitting with you when you receive the call and now you've got to talk over your decision with them.

**HAWAIIAN VACATION!
ALL EXPENSES PAID!**

Enjoy the trip of your dreams
Includes:
Roundtrip Airfare!
First Class Accomodations!
Native Hawaiian Dinner with Dancing!
Free Scuba Diving Lessons!
AND MORE!

6. A teenager was supposed to be home by midnight but arrives home at 3:00 A.M. The teenager doesn't want to get caught coming in so late, so he or she tries to tiptoe quietly into the house. A younger brother, however, was hungry and came downstairs to get something to eat. The teenager and the brother bump right into each other, making a lot of noise and waking up the parents. The parents express their anger and concerns as the children try to explain their actions.

▲ "So you thought I wouldn't wake up, huh?"

7. You are on an airplane taking the first vacation you've had in two years. You try to start a conversation with an interesting person next to you, but a naughty child is making a lot of noise and keeps interrupting you. The parent of the child doesn't seem to care and does nothing to control the child.

FOCUS

TOEFL® iBT

Digressions in Lectures

In Part 2 of this chapter, you learned about digressions. Lectures on the TOEFL® iBT include many digressions to imitate the style of real academic lectures.

Questions on the TOEFL® iBT do not ask about the material in a digression—its content is not important. However, some listening questions ask what a speaker means by using a certain transition phrase. Such questions may target expressions that begin or end a digression because they relate to a speaker's purposes in saying certain things.

1 **Transition Phrases: Lecture** Listen to the lecture about group work and take notes. Pay special attention to transition phrases that are related to digressions. Then answer the questions.

1. Listen again to part of the lecture.

    What does the professor mean when he says, "just kidding"?

    (A) "That comment is only for young people."

    (B) "That is not what I meant to say."

    (C) "That was only a joke."

    (D) "That comment is very true."

2. Why does the professor say, "seriously"?

    (A) to end a funny digression

    (B) to begin a serious digression

    (C) to tell students to pay attention

    (D) to tell students to stop laughing

3. Listen again to part of the lecture.

   Why does the professor say, "by the way"?

     Ⓐ to introduce a method of thinking

     Ⓑ to introduce a return to the topic

     Ⓒ to introduce a minor point about the topic

     Ⓓ to introduce the source of information

4. What does the professor mean when he says, "well, never mind"?

     Ⓐ "Please do not be offended by this."

     Ⓑ "Please do not think about this."

     Ⓒ "That idea is off the main topic."

     Ⓓ "That idea is hard to remember."

5. Listen again to part of the lecture.

   What does the professor indicate by saying, "but let me get to that later"?

     Ⓐ The topic is unimportant.

     Ⓑ The topic is a high priority right now.

     Ⓒ Other things must be discussed now.

     Ⓓ Stop asking questions about low-priority topics.

Self-Assessment Log

Check (✓) the words in this chapter you have acquired and can use in your daily life.

Nouns	Verbs	Adjective	Expression
▦ eye contact	▦ recap	▦ random	▦ pretty much
▦ field of interest	▦ wind		
▦ identity			

Check (✓) your level of accomplishment for the skills introduced in this chapter. How comfortable do you feel using these skills?

	Very comfortable	Somewhat comfortable	Not at all comfortable
Recognizing digressions	☐	☐	☐
Recognizing returns from digressions to the main topic	☐	☐	☐
Recognizing the intonation patterns of the three types of tag questions and understanding their meaning	☐	☐	☐
Using tag questions to ask for information	☐	☐	☐
Using tag questions to ask for confirmation	☐	☐	☐
Using tag questions to challenge	☐	☐	☐

Think about the topics and activities in this chapter and complete the statements.

In this chapter, I learned something new about _____

_____

_____

I especially liked (topic or activity) _____

_____

_____

I would like to know more about _____

_____

_____

10 Crime and Punishment

"Character—the willingness to accept responsibility for one's own life—is the source from which self-respect springs."

Joan Didion
U.S. novelist

In this
CHAPTER

Lecture Human Choice—Predetermination or Free Will?

Learning Strategy Paraphrasing

Language Function Wishes, Hopes, and Desires

 Connecting to the Topic

1. What are three things that are against the law, and what are the punishments usually given for each of these in your community?

2. Which of these punishments do you think are fair? Why?

3. Which punishments are not fair? Why?

Did You Know?

- On December 1, 1955, Rosa Parks, a 42-year-old African-American seamstress, chose to break the law in Montgomery, Alabama. She was ordered by a city bus driver to give up her seat to a white man, as was required by the city's racial segregation laws that kept the races apart. She refused to give up her seat and was arrested. Four days later, the African-American community, led by Dr. Martin Luther King, Jr., began a boycott of the city bus company and refused to ride the buses. The boycott lasted 382 days. Finally, the U.S. Supreme Court ruled that racial segregation on city buses was unconstitutional. Because of her role in starting the successful boycott, Rosa Parks became known as the "mother of the civil rights movement."

▲ Rosa Parks (1913–2005)

- The longest known prison sentence ever given out by a judge was 141,078 years. A Thai woman and seven associates each received this sentence in the Bangkok Criminal Court in 1989. Their crime: cheating the public through a fake deposit-taking business.

- Studies of the death penalty in the United States show that, contrary to expectations, states that use the death penalty as punishment for the crime of murder have higher murder rates than states that do not use it.

1 **What Do You Think?** Take turns speaking about each of the following with a partner.

1. Rosa Parks broke a state law and was put in jail. Later the courts decided that this law was unconstitutional and she became a hero. Do you think she made the best choice? Do you think everyone should break the law if they think it is unfair? Why or why not?

2. The Thai court sent a woman and her friends to prison for more years than they could possibly live. Do you think this type of punishment works to stop people from committing crimes? Why or why not?

Sharing Your Experience

2 **Wrongs You've Done or Considered Doing** Answer these questions in small groups. Then share one or two stories from your group with the whole class.

1. Have you ever done or considered doing something you knew was wrong in order to get something you wanted? For example, have you ever pretended to be sick in order to get a day off, or taken something from a store without paying for it? What was the wrong that you did or considered doing? If you did the wrong, what was the result? If you didn't do it, why didn't you do it?

2. Have you ever considered doing something that was against the law or rules because it felt "right" to you (as Rosa Park did)? What was the result?

Vocabulary Preview

3 **Guessing Definitions** You will hear these words in the lecture on human behavior. Try to figure out their definitions in small groups. Share your knowledge of words or parts of words with your group. Write the letter of the correct definition beside each word.

Words

1. _____ free will
2. _____ karma
3. _____ life-and-death
4. _____ predetermination
5. _____ programmed
6. _____ reincarnation
7. _____ remorse
8. _____ violation

Definitions

a. the rebirth of spirits or souls into new bodies or forms of life

b. controlled to do a certain thing or behave a certain way automatically and without thinking

c. a wrongdoing, a serious mistake, or something illegal

d. the regret or bad feeling you have for doing something wrong

e. the freedom that humans have to make choices and guide their own fates or destinies

f. the belief that all events in a person's life have already been decided

g. the philosophy that the good and bad things we do determine what will happen to us in the future and in our next lives

h. very important, as if your life depends on it

PART 2 Paraphrasing

Strategy

Paraphrasing What an Instructor Says

Paraphrasing is restating an idea using different words. In class, you may be asked to restate in your own words something the instructor said or that you read. Paraphrasing is a useful study skill because it helps you remember ideas and concepts that you learn.

Before You Listen

1 **Considering the Topic** Predetermination and free will are key concepts that will be discussed by the lecturer.

- Read the following list of activities and think carefully about each one. Which ones do you freely choose? Which ones do you not get to choose? Decide whether each one is an example of free will or predetermination and put a check in the corresponding column. Add at least one item to the list for each category.
- Discuss your responses in small groups.
- Share the highlights of your discussion with the whole class. Did you agree about most items? Did your group discussion cause you to change your opinions in any way?

Activity	Predetermination	Free will
going to the movies		
going to school		
how you travel to school		
choosing a marriage partner		
whether to work or not		
your nationality		
your religion		

2 **Practice Paraphrasing** Using your own words, rewrite the following sentences. They contain ideas covered in the lecture you will hear in this chapter. Do not use your dictionary. Try to get the meanings of words from the sentences and make educated guesses. Compare answers with your classmates. Use a dictionary *only* if there are important differences among the answers.

Example "The unexamined life is not worth living." —Socrates

If you don't look closely at your own behavior, your life will be

meaningless.

1. Maybe we are programmed to do the things we do.

   _____

   _____

   _____

2. If you feel that you are not in control, then you might also feel that you do not have to take responsibility for your choices.

   _____

   _____

   _____

3. Our relationship to the past and to the future seems to be connected with our present choices.

   _____

   _____

   _____

4. The practical implications of choice increase and intensify when life-and-death decisions have to be made.

   _____

   _____

   _____

5. We only punish people who choose consciously, willfully, and freely to commit crimes.

   _____

   _____

   _____

3 Listening to Paraphrase Parts of a Lecture Listen to the lecture and paraphrase, or restate, the following sections. Your teacher will stop the recording after each section.

1. Listen and paraphrase what the professor says about predetermination and free will.

_____

_____

_____

_____

_____

2. Listen and paraphrase what the professor says about decisions involving criminal offenses. Pay special attention to the example of a judge sentencing a person to prison for violating the rules of a community.

_____

_____

_____

_____

_____

3. Listen and paraphrase what the professor says about John Hinckley, Jr., who was not sent to prison for his actions.

_____

_____

_____

_____

_____

4. Listen and paraphrase what the professor says about the everyday choices we all have to make, and the professor's final comments.

_____

_____

_____

_____

_____

4 **Comparing Notes** Share your answers from Activity 3 in small groups by reading them aloud. How did your praphrasing differ from that of your classmates? You may want to listen to the lecture again before and after this activity to check your answers.

5 **Paraphrasing Problems for Group Discussion** Real-life situations often force us to make unpleasant choices and to give up things we want. Work in small groups to paraphrase and discuss the following difficult situations. Use these guidelines to structure your paraphrasing practice.

1. Only one person in the group looks at the textbook for each situation. This person reads one of the problem situations silently and then paraphrases it for the group. Do not mention the possible solutions given in the book at this time.

2. All group members then paraphrase and clarify what the problem is and discuss what they would do about it and why.

3. The first person then reads aloud the possible solutions given in the book. The group discusses the pros and cons of any of these solutions that group members did not mention earlier.

4. Another person takes the textbook, chooses another problem from the list, and repeats Steps 1–3, making sure that each person has at least one opportunity to practice paraphrasing.

Problem Situations

1. You're eating dinner at your favorite restaurant. When a couple is being seated at a table next to you, you notice that the tip that the last customer left for the server is still on the table. As soon as the couple is alone, the man puts the tip in his pocket.

   What would you do?

   (A) gently remind the man that the money belongs to the server

   (B) quietly tell your server

   (C) call the police on your cell phone

   (D) nothing

2. You're standing in the checkout line in a market when you notice a person in the line next to you take two small candy bars out of the shopping basket and put them into his or her coat pocket.

   What would you do?

   (A) tell the person to pay for them

   (B) tell the checkout clerk what just happened

   (C) clear your throat and stare at the person

   (D) ignore the situation

3. A course you are taking is extremely difficult. Your friend, who took the same course last semester, says that the final is absolutely impossible but that you might pass it with a little "help"—that is, if your friend tells you what will be on the test.

What would you do?

(A) let your friend give you the answers to the test

(B) let your friend give you some hints but not tell you all the answers

(C) not accept any help from your friend

(D) report your friend's offer to the instructor

4. You work in a large company and are in charge of hiring new employees. You must choose a new office manager from two candidates. One is a long-time friend who is new to the company; the other is a first-rate worker who has been with the company for eight years.

What would you do?

(A) offer your friend the position

(B) offer the long-term, first-rate employee the job

(C) look for a third candidate from outside the company

(D) resign from the company and look for a new job

5. The speed limit on the highway is 55 mph. All the cars around you are going at least 65 or 70 mph, so you decide to move along with the rest of the traffic at about 68 mph. All of a sudden, you hear a siren and see the swirling lights of a police car behind you. You pull over to the side of the road with the police car right behind you. The police officer asks you why you were going so fast.

What would you say?

(A) I was staying with the flow of traffic.

(B) Why did you stop me? That guy in the Porsche was going even faster (not true).

(C) I'm sorry. I'm a foreigner and I don't understand the laws here (not true).

(D) I'm sorry, but I'm on the way to the hospital to see a very sick relative (not true).

▲ "Is there a problem, officer?"

PART 3   Wishes, Hopes, and Desires

Strategy

Understanding and Expressing Wishes, Hopes, and Desires
The lecturer in this chapter wants his students to seriously consider the choices they make and the underlying reasons for these choices. He uses a variety of expressions to indicate wishes, hopes, and desires during the lecture, including the following:

Ways to Express Wishes, Hopes, and Desires

*I wish…	I want…
*If only…	I need…
**I hope…	I could use…

Wish is used for things that are less likely to occur. Therefore, *wish* is used with conditional verb forms. (*If only* has a similar function to *wish*.)
**Hope* is used for things that are more likely to happen.

NOTE: Often, our choice of words says a lot about how we feel, even if we don't realize it. When we use *wish* and *if only*, we express a somewhat more pessimistic view. *Hope* expresses a more optimistic view. Contrast the following examples:

I wish I were a famous athlete.
I hope I can be successful.

If only I could fly like a bird.
I hope I pass my pilot exam.

1 **Listening for Wishes, Hopes, and Desires** Listen for expressions of wishes, hopes, and desires in the following conversation. Write down all the expressions you hear. Compare notes with your classmates.

_____

_____

_____

_____

_____

_____

_____

_____

▲ Making some easy money for quick deliveries

2 **Listening to Paraphrase Wishes, Hopes, and Desires** Read the following six items before you listen to the lecture once more. Then listen for the expressions in italics that are used in the lecture and complete the sentences, using your own words to paraphrase the lecturer. Stop the recording if necessary.

1. The lecturer *hopes* that by the end of class, the students understand

_____

_____

_____

2. The lecturer *wants* to hear the students' ideas about

_____

_____

_____

3. The lecturer asks the students how many of them have looked at their past actions and said, "I *wish…*"

_____

_____

_____

4. or "*If only…*"

_____

_____

_____

5. The lecturer does not want to focus on Hinckley's punishment; he *wants*

_____

_____

_____

_____

6. In summary, he *hopes* the lecture

_____

_____

_____

_____

▲ John Hinckley was found "not guilty by reason of insanity" of his attempt to assassinate President Ronald Reagan.

3 **Expressing Hopes and Wishes** Complete the following sentences. Then share your answers in small groups.

1. I wish I were _____.

2. All I really need is _____.

3. If only I could _____.

4. I want to make better choices in my life. I hope to do this by _____

_____.

Talk It Over

4 **Expressing your Hopes and Wishes, Optimism and Pessimism**
Role-play the following three situations with a partner. Use a variety of expressions from the list on page 173 to express your wishes and hopes. Be careful not to sound demanding and impolite. Present one situation to the whole class.

Situation 1

It is the first day of a course on criminal law. You've been hoping to take the class for a long time, but you haven't had the time or the money to do it until now. The instructor begins the class by asking you to explain what you hope to get from the course.

Situation 2

Lucky you! You have been selected for a job interview for a position as a translator for the World Court. The interviewer asks what you hope to gain from your experience as a translator. You ask the interviewer what qualities she or he hopes to find in an employee.

▲ World Court in session

Situation 3

You are hoping to finish your studies this year, but the university changed the requirements for graduation last year and now you will have to take another course. You decide to discuss your options with the dean of your department.

5 **A "Wishes" and "Hopes" Drama** In groups, role-play interviews about the following situation, with each person choosing a different character (or two) and expressing the wishes and hopes of the various people involved. You can use phrases like these:

> I wish...
> If only he...
> I hope...
>
> He needs...
> He could use...

Situation

Charles Burke is on trial for murder. He was a wonderful child and did well in school. At age 19, he was drafted into the army and was sent to fight in Afghanistan. Two years later he returned home and tried to pick up where he'd left off, but things were never the same again for Charles.

He became angry easily and he was soon thrown out of school for fighting with a professor. He was fired from several jobs. He wanted to meet a nice girl and get married, but he couldn't seem to get close to anyone. Finally, one day Charles shot someone "for no reason."

Charles's lawyer hopes that Charles will not be held responsible for his crime. He hopes that the judge and jury will understand that at the moment of the shooting, Charles did not know right from wrong, that he was temporarily insane and did not consciously choose to commit murder.

The following people are being interviewed by the TV news network, CNN:

- Charles Burke
- Charles's lawyer
- The prosecuting attorney
- Charles's mother or father
- A dismissed jury member who was released in the middle of the trial and is now allowed to give interviews to the news media

- Charles's best friend from school
- Charles's kind grade-school teacher
- The judge
- The wife of the murdered man

FOCUS

Idea-Connection Questions

The listening section of the TOEFL® iBT contains some questions about connections among the ideas in a lecture or conversation. To answer correctly, you need to have a mental picture of the flow of ideas. You also must see how several ideas combine to make a larger point.

These questions come in two formats. They may be either ordinary multiple-choice questions or "table" questions. Table questions ask you to click on certain boxes to categorize ideas from the passage. You have already practiced answering table questions in this chapter and in several other chapters. The following sample question refers to this chapter's lecture about human choice.

Sample Table Question

In the lecture, some of the professor's examples are meant to illustrate free will and others are meant to illustrate predetermination. Indicate which principle each of the following illustrates. Click in the proper box for each example.

	Free Will	Predetermination
The concept of *karma*	X	
Decisions made by a spiritual force		X
Jean Valjean's crime	X	

1 Idea-Connection Questions: Lecture Close your books and listen to the lecture about chemicals and crime. Take notes. Then open your books and answer the idea-connection questions that follow.

1. According to the professor, what was one of the first indications of a connection between serotonin levels and violent behavior?

    Ⓐ the case of Jason

    Ⓑ research that led to the development of SSRIs

    Ⓒ the case of a Dutch family

    Ⓓ research that led to the development of MAOA

2. In the lecture, the professor mentions some support for the belief that people freely choose whether to commit a crime or not. She also mentions arguments for the opposite—a lack of free choice. Indicate which position each statement supports. Mark an *X* in the proper box for each statement.

	Free Choice	No Free Choice
Brain chemistry influences decisions but doesn't make them.		
A person cannot control brain chemistry.		
Some criminals are judged legally insane.		
People have to overcome their chemical limitations.		

3. According to the professor, why is it sometimes helpful to reduce the speed at which serotonin is absorbed by brain cells?

   Ⓐ because high levels of un-absorbed serotonin can be harmful

   Ⓑ because low levels of un-absorbed serotonin can be harmful

   Ⓒ because high levels of SSRIs in the brain can be harmful

   Ⓓ because low levels of SSRIs in the brain can be harmful

4. Why does the professor start the lecture by mentioning free will and predetermination?

   Ⓐ because higher powers may influence human decisions

   Ⓑ because humans freely choose what to do

   Ⓒ because body chemistry might influence human choices

   Ⓓ because no one has debates about human choice anymore

Self-Assessment Log

Check (✓) the words in this chapter you have acquired and can use in your daily life.

Nouns
- free will
- karma
- predetermination
- reincarnation
- remorse
- violation

Adjective
- programmed

Idiom
- life-and-death

Check (✓) your level of accomplishment for the skills introduced in this chapter. How comfortable do you feel using these skills?

	Very comfortable	Somewhat comfortable	Not at all comfortable
Paraphrasing	☐	☐	☐
Understanding expressions of wishes, hopes, and desires	☐	☐	☐
Using *wish*, *hope*, and *if only* appropriately to express wishes, hopes, and desires	☐	☐	☐

Think about the topics and activities in this chapter and complete the statements.

In this chapter, I learned something new about _____

_____

_____

I especially liked (topic or activity) _____

_____

_____

I would like to know more about _____

_____

_____

Audioscript

PART 2 Listening to Make
Predictions

2 Listening to Make Predictions
page 10

Presentation: Don't Lecture Me: A New
Paradigm for the University of the Future

Professor: Good morning! I am Jack Miller,
and welcome to our university.

Students: Good morning. Hello. Hi.

Professor: Before I begin my presentation
about the very unique program we have here,
I'd like to hear from all of you. What does the
title of my presentation "Don't Lecture Me:
A New Paradigm for the University of the
Future" bring to mind? What does it make you
think about? Just call out your questions.

Student 1: Why not lecture? I mean, it's as
good a way to learn as any, right?

Professor: Good question. Any others?

Student 2: Who decided that *how* we learn
what we learn will affect our future success?

Professor: Interesting. Next?

Student 3: How does the program here differ
from a traditional university program?

Professor: Good, got that. Yes, go ahead.

Student 4: Is this one of those programs that
centers around group projects? If so, what about
individual accountability? And grades? Can I
get into a good graduate school from here?

Professor: Excellent point. Hmm. Any
more? No? Then let's begin with the first
question. Why not lecture? Well, experts say
that lectures have outlived their usefulness.
You see, research shows that it's impossible
to remember all of the information presented
during a typical lecture. But this presents us
with a paradox. On the one hand, lectures are
still the primary way university courses are
taught. It's what both students and professors

are used to. On the other hand, they are not
efficacious. OK so far?

I see a few puzzled looks. What I mean is
that lectures may be what you're accustomed
to, but they are not the most effective way to
learn. They simply do not produce great results
and we are finding that students are learning
in spite of lectures, not because of them. Does
that make sense to you?

Student 2: I think so. I remember that when I
took an astronomy class in high school, I had
so much trouble remembering everything that
the teacher told us in her lectures and kept
failing the quizzes. But when I joined the
astronomy club and started actually looking
at stars and talking to my friends about what
we were seeing, my test scores got much,
much better.

Professor: That's right! Exactly! And here's
something else to consider. With modern
technology, if all you needed were lectures,
we could just get professors to do each of their
lectures once and then put them on the web.
So you can see the problem, right?

Students: Sure. Right. Uh-huh. And then fire
the faculty. Yes, very funny!

Professor: OK, so who decided that we needed
a new paradigm for learning? Who decided
that *how* you learn is more important to your
success in the future than what you learn? Well,
it was, as it is with most important revelations,
not just one or even a few individuals who
came to this same conclusion, but many, many.

It may surprise you, but educational
philosophers and researchers have been trying
to shake up the traditional educational system
for generations. In fact, the University of
California at Santa Cruz, established in 1965,
eliminated large lecture classes (with 100 or
even 200 students), in favor of more intimate
classes of only 30 students that allowed students
to talk and not just listen. They also used
a portfolio system where students submitted
a portfolio, or file, of original work instead
of taking traditional tests. Then the work
was evaluated using a narrative or descriptive
system instead of traditional grading. And the
program at Alverno College in Milwaukee,

established as a traditional womens' college in 1887, has been transformed by some very enlightened educators into an ability-based integrated curriculum that focuses on problem-solving skills, group skills, and community skills, as equally as important as the retention of various "facts." Are you following me?

Student 5: Maybe. Sort of.

Professor: OK. Let me put it this way. Both UC Santa Cruz and Alverno College are examples of programs that focus more on developing students' interests in and capacities for learning and communicating in a changing world than on the number of bits of factual information they can memorize today. Their goal is to provide students with the tools they need to succeed in a world in which the information that they might memorize today could be totally obsolete in the future. Did you get that?

Students: Maybe. Not exactly. I'm not sure.

Professor: All right. I know that these ideas might be totally foreign to some of you. I think my colleague Stephen Lehmkuhle, the chancellor at the new University of Minnesota campus in Rochester, may have explained these nontraditional educational ideas best in a recent interview. He said that he is trying to create a university of the future that, as he puts it, "prepares students for jobs that don't yet exist, to solve problems that aren't yet known, using technologies that have not yet been invented."

So we're back to where we started. Why doesn't the traditional lecture format work to accomplish these goals? Perhaps if we move on to the third question that was asked, "How does our program differ from a traditional one?" it will become more obvious to you. Our program has been greatly influenced by all three of the programs that I've mentioned, UC Santa Cruz, Alverno, and especially the very new University of Minnesota Rochester and is totally based on a set of student learning outcomes and objectives rather than merely on faculty interests. Did you catch the most important point here?

Student 3: I think I see where you're going with this. Are you saying that the faculty here will never create a course on a topic on which they just happen to be doing research and then require us to pass tests on lectures on this topic?

Professor: Yes, exactly! But there's more to it than that. Additionally, our program actually rewards faculty for effective teaching as well as research—and that includes research on student learning as well as in their own areas of expertise. Furthermore, we, just as at both Alverno and UM Rochester, have an integrated curriculum. This means that your biology professor might be collaborating with your English professor, and key concepts that you learn in one class will be reinforced in new contexts in another class. Got it?

Student 3: Well, yes, for the most part. But I think there's still a bit of a problem.

Professor: OK. What do you think that might be?

Student 3: Well, for one thing, this approach ignores the fact that for some of us, lectures are what we're used to, and we know how to study for those kinds of tests, even if we do forget everything the next day. What if I can't figure out what's expected of me here?

Professor: Oh, I'm glad you asked that! Let me tell you about an aspect of our program that I think is truly awesome. We have three types of faculty members here, just as they do at UM Rochester: 1) those that are hired to design curriculum as well as teach in their fields; 2) those that implement or teach the curriculum and meet with students very frequently outside of class; and 3) those that serve as "success coaches" or academic and career advisors only.

Student 4: That sounds great! Uh... Do you have time to address my question about group work and grading? I understand that group projects are often part of a program like this one.

Professor: Right! That's very true. We do expect you to learn how to work together, to collaborate, to communicate, and to connect, just as you will be expected to do out in the world, at your first job, in your communities and at home. We don't, however, rely on group grades on group projects to evaluate progress. You will all be individually accountable for meeting clearly explained goals and objectives, but you can be assured that there will be no surprise quizzes on seemingly irrelevant information, just because it's quicker to grade.

Oh, I see our time is up. Time for our lunch break. In our afternoon orientation session, please be prepared to share some of your own positive educational experiences. And I don't just mean your experiences in classes. Please think about those experiences outside of classes that were powerful and how we can bring those into our curriculum here. OK then. The cafeteria is just down the hall, first door on your right. See you after lunch.

PART 3   Offering and Requesting Clarification

1   Listening for Tone of Voice   page 17

Conversation 1

Ms. Torres: To help the passengers disembark in an emergency, you will have to first, stay calm; second, speak loudly, but do not scream; and thirdly, keep instructions short and to the point. Is that clear?

Conversation 2

Mrs. Gobel: No, you can't talk to friends on Facebook tonight. First, you have to help your father with the yard work, help me fix dinner, finish your homework, take a bath, brush your teeth, and then go to bed before 10:00. Is that clear?

2   Listening for Expressions that Offer Clarification   page 17

See Part 2 Listening to Make Predictions on page 180 of this audioscript.

4   Requesting Clarification During a Lecture or Presentation   page 19

See Part 2 Listening to Make Predictions on page 180 of this audioscript.

PART 4   Focus on Testing

1   Pragmatic Understanding: Presentation   page 21

1. _Listen again to part of the presentation._

Student 4: Is this one of those programs that centers around group projects? If so, what about individual accountability? And grades? Can I get into a good graduate school from here?

Professor: Excellent point. Hmm. Any more? No?

Question 1: Why does the professor say, "Any more? No?"

2. _Listen again to part of the presentation._

Professor: You see, research shows that it's impossible to remember all of the information presented during a typical lecture. But this presents us with a paradox. On the one hand, lectures are still the primary way university courses are taught. It's what both students and professors are used to. On the other hand, they are not efficacious.

Question 2: What is the professor's opinion about lectures?

Question 3: How do you think the professor would answer the student's question, "Can I get into a good graduate school from here?"

4. _Listen again to part of the presentation._

Professor: In fact, the University of California at Santa Cruz, established in 1965, eliminated large lecture classes (with 100 or even 200 students) in favor of more intimate classes of only 30 students that allowed students to talk and not just listen. They also used a portfolio system where students submitted a portfolio or file of original work instead of taking traditional tests. Then the work was evaluated using a narrative or descriptive system instead of traditional grading. And the program at Alverno College in Milwaukee, established as a traditional womens' college in 1887, has been transformed by some very enlightened educators into an ability-based integrated curriculum that focuses on problem-solving skills, group skills and community skills, as equally important as the retention of various "facts."

Question 4: Why does the professor mention UC Santa Cruz and Alverno College?

5. _Listen again to part of the presentation._

Professor: Our program… is based on a set of student learning outcomes and objective rather than merely on faculty interests.

Question 5: What is the professor implying in this statement?

PART 2 Distinguishing Main Ideas and Supporting Details

3 Listening for Main Ideas and Supporting Information page 31

4 Constructing an Outline page 31

Lecture: Penguin Partners at the Pole

Professor Gill: Good morning.

Students: Good morning. Hello. Hi.

Professor Gill: Well, to continue with our study of the ecosystem of Antarctica, I have invited a special guest to speak to you today. My colleague, Professor Byrd, has just returned from a two-year field study in Antarctica and he's going to share a few things about a part-time polar resident—the penguin.

Professor Byrd: Hello. I see that you're all smiling. It never fails! Every time people hear that my lecture will be about penguins, everyone immediately seems happier. This is not surprising. No one can resist these awkward little creatures that appear to be dressed in black and white suits. Well, to begin. Antarctica is like a huge and desolate icy desert and only the strongest forms of life survive there. It seems strange that this hard land could be the spring and summer home of a migratory bird—the penguin.

Did I say bird? It also seems strange to call something that cannot fly a bird. But that's not all! The penguin is a tireless swimmer and is also affectionate, considerate, and loyal—rare qualities in the bird kingdom. Because of their warm, friendly, and cooperative natures, these lovely birds are thought of as the treasure of Antarctica.

The penguin is an extremely important part of a very limited ecosystem. In the Antarctic, all of the activity of the ecosystem takes place on a thin shelf of land next to the great dome of ice that covers most of the region. It is here, to this little bit of beachfront, that one species of penguin comes to mate and raise babies. It would be a little cold for us at this beach, though.

Students: That's for sure. Absolutely

Professor Byrd: Today I'm going to talk about only one type of penguin, the Adélie penguin. The Adélie penguin arrives in the relative warmth of spring, when the temperature rises above zero degrees Fahrenheit. That would be about minus seventeen degrees Celsius. Right away the penguin begins a long fast, a time when it does not eat. During the previous months, the penguins continuously eat krill— small, shrimplike animals—and small fish in warmer waters, and in the spring, they have a store of fat to help them survive the months ahead. Using these fat reserves, they are able to swim hundreds of miles through freezing waters back to the familiar shore of Antarctica each spring.

When the penguins arrive at the nesting ground, their first task is to pair up—to mate— and to begin a kind of "civilized" life. Since as many as 50,000 birds may gather at a time, there is definitely a need for order and neatness. Because of this need for order, penguins build nests in perfect rows and the nesting area looks very much like the streets of a city.

This organization and order, however, is often interrupted by battles or fights between birds. For example, two male birds may fight a small war over a particularly adorable female that they think will make a good "wife". Or a male and a female may battle as they settle the marriage contract and reach agreement on when and how they will mate and where they will build their nest. These little battles can go on constantly for several weeks, until all of the pairs have settled down. The penguins never actually kill one another, but it is not unusual to see bloodstains and broken wings.

The male winner of the love battle over a female wins a relationship with the female that is one of the most extraordinary in the animal world. There seems to be a wonderful understanding between mates. I've observed the delicate and kind way they treat each other, standing very close and swaying back and forth as if they are dancing to celebrate their marriage. The losers, the males that fail to find a suitable mate, move to the edge of the nesting ground. These birds become the "hooligans," or minor troublemakers of the group. They steal unguarded eggs, disturb nests, and play jokes on the happy couples.

Student 1: I think we have a few of those hooligan types in this class.

Students: (laughing)

Professor Byrd: Yes, I've seen that behavior myself. So… after nearly a month of fasting, the eggs are laid in little nests made of stones by the males. Then family life begins. Although the parenting instinct is very strong and parental care is truly dedicated and careful, as many as 75 percent of the eggs are lost due to catastrophic floods, deaths of the parents, destruction of the nests by landslides or heavy snows, bad behavior of the "hooligan" males I mentioned before and, of course, there are the skuas—the predatory birds that come down from the sky to eat the eggs and even baby penguins.

Students: That's awful! That's so sad! Oh, no!

Professor Byrd: Yes, that's sad, but some eggs do survive, of course, and once the chicks, the baby penguins, begin to hatch out of the eggs, the penguin colony teems with life. The long fast is over, and the parents take turns feeding and bringing back food for their new penguin chick.

It is during this period that we can see the comical character of the penguin. They often go off to feed in large groups, walking or sliding in single file lines on their way from their nesting ground to the ocean. At the shoreline, they dare one another to jump into the water. They often approach the edge of a cliff and then retreat over and over again, until finally, one brave penguin dives in. Then the others follow almost at once, jumping into the water from exactly the same spot on the shore. In the water, they play various water sports that they've invented while they fill themselves up with krill and other small sea animals.

It's not all fun and games, however. Even though their black and white color helps hide them, there is not very much the penguins can do to protect themselves from the jaws of the sea leopard. This scary creature looks like a cross between a seal and a great white shark. Some of you might remember the movie *Jaws*?

Students: Yeah! Sure! Right!

Student 1: Sure we do! Dah-dum, dah-dum, dah-dum!

Students: (laughing)

Professor Byrd: Well, the sea leopard's jaw is as tough as the great white shark's. The sea leopard is really a large seal with many large, sharp teeth, an aggressive disposition, and a taste for penguin meat. Even though penguins are excellent swimmers, it is difficult for them to escape these ferocious predators.

For this reason, the group of feeding penguins is smaller when it returns to the nesting ground. But penguins are generous creatures and food is shared with the orphaned chicks—the chicks whose parents have been killed. Adult penguins also share babysitting duties. One bird will watch over several chicks while the others play.

Student 2: Even the males?

Professor Byrd: Especially the males!

Student 2: Hear that, you guys?

Students: (laughing)

Professor Byrd: Oh, yes. Penguins share everything. And they love to visit with neighbors, explore nearby ice floes or islands, and even climb mountains, following the leader in long lines up the mountainside.

When the mating season finally ends, the penguins line up in rows like little black and white soldiers and prepare to march to the sea. Responding to a signal that humans cannot perceive, the penguins suddenly begin their highly organized and orderly walk. At the edge of the sea, they stand as if at attention again, waiting for another signal. When it is given, they begin their swim back to their winter home on another part of the continent.

Well, I think I'm keeping you a bit late. If Professor Gill will invite me back, maybe we can continue talking about the penguins another time.

Students: Yes! That would be great! Please do come back, Professor!

Professor Gill: Definitely. Please do come back. Thank you so much, Professor Byrd. We all enjoyed your talk tremendously.

Conversation 1

Driver: Pardon me. How do I get to the university library?

Police officer: You make a U-turn, go back on Washington until you hit Jefferson, about three blocks, then make a right turn, and it's the second white building on your left.

Driver: Could you repeat that, please?

Police officer: Sure. You make a U-turn, go back on Washington until you hit Jefferson, about three blocks, then make a right turn, and it's the second white building on your left.

Driver: You mean I turn around and stay on Washington until I get to Jefferson and then make a right?

Police officer: Yeah, that's right.

Driver: And did you say it's a white building on the left?

Police officer: Uh-huh.

Driver: Thanks a lot.

Police officer: You're welcome.

Conversation 2

Student: I didn't get the directions on the test. That's why I didn't do well.

Professor: Well, Tim, the directions say, "Answer 1A and then choose and answer 1B, 1C, or 1D."

Student: Do you mean to say that we had to do A and then choose either B, C, or D?

Professor: Yes, you had a choice for the second half of the question.

Student: Oh, OK.

Conversation 3

Student: Professor Thompson, I'm not sure I understand the directions on this test.

Professor: Well, Tim, the directions say, "Answer 1A and then choose and answer 1B, 1C, or 1D."

Student: You mean that we all do 1A, but then we each could do any one of 1B, C, or D?

Professor: That's right, Tim.

Student: Oh, now I see. Thank you.

Conversation 4

Student: What do I do now?

Assistant: You take that white sheet and the blue card. You fill out the white sheet with the courses you want. Then you have your advisor sign the white sheet and the blue card, and you turn them in to the first-floor office in Building Four and pay your fees.

Student: You mean I've got to have my advisor sign both the sheet and the card, and then I've got to stand in line again?

Conversation 5

Student: Excuse me, could you tell me what I must do next to pre-register?

Assistant: You take that white sheet and the blue card. You fill out the white sheet with the courses you want. Then you have your advisor sign the white sheet and the blue card, and you turn them in to the first-floor office in Building Four and pay your fees.

Student: I'm not sure I understand. Do you mean that the advisor must sign both forms? And that I take the forms to Building Four and pay my fees there?

Assistant: Yes, that's right.

Student: Oh, OK. Now I understand. Thank you.

See Part 2 Distinguishing Main Ideas and Supporting Details on page 183 of this audioscript.

Conversation 1

Speaker: Wow, Frank! You mean you're taking French 4, Biology 2, Intro to Economics, Eastern Religions, Music Appreciation, and Beginning Acting? That's a really heavy load for your first semester.

Question: What is the speaker implying?

Conversation 2

Speaker: I can't believe this! I'm spending over $2,000 a year for this meal plan, and it doesn't include meals on Saturdays and Sundays!

Question: How is this student feeling and why?

② **Pragmatic Understanding: Lecture**
page 40

1. Listen again to part of the lecture.

Professor Byrd: It seems strange that this hard land could be the spring and summer home of a migratory bird—the penguin. Did I say bird? It also seems strange to call something that cannot fly a bird.

Question 1: Why does the professor say, "Did I say bird?"

2. Listen again to part of the lecture.

Professor Byrd: In the Antarctic, all of the activity of the ecosystem takes place on a thin shelf of land next to the great dome of ice that covers most of the region. It is here, to this little bit of beachfront, that one species of penguin comes to mate and raise babies. It would be a little cold for us at this beach, though.

Question 2: What is the professor's opinion about the penguin's choice of a home site?

3. Listen again to part of the lecture.

Professor Byrd: The losers, the males that fail to find a suitable mate, move to the edge of the nesting ground. These birds become the "hooligans," or minor troublemakers of the group. They steal unguarded eggs, disturb nests, and play jokes on the happy couples.

Student 1: I think we have a few of those hooligan types in this class.

Question 3: What is the student implying by saying, "I think we have a few of those hooligans in this class"?

4. Listen again to part of the lecture.

Professor Byrd: It's not all fun and games, however. Even though their black and white color helps hide them, there is not very much the penguins can do to protect themselves from the jaws of the sea leopard. This scary creature looks like a cross between a seal and a great white shark. Some of you might remember the movie *Jaws*?

Question 4: Why does the professor mention the movie *Jaws*?

5. Listen again to part of the lecture.

Professor Byrd: Adult penguins also share babysitting duties. One bird will watch over several chicks while the others play.

Student 2: Even the males?

Professor Byrd: Especially the males!

Student 2: Hear that, you guys?

Question 5: Why does the student say, "Hear that, you guys?"

CHAPTER **3** **Relationships**

PART 2 Understanding Straw Man Arguments

③ Listening for Straw Man Arguments
page 50

④ Listening for Data and Details Refuting Straw Man Arguments
page 50

Lecture: Mom Always Liked You Best

Professor: Good morning. Welcome to the fourth session of our seminar on family dynamics. Before I introduce the topic for today's discussion, I'd like to ask you a question. What do you think is likely to be the longest relationship in your life? I mean the one that lasts for the greatest number of years. Ah, you smile… think you know the answer to this one, do you? OK… go ahead. Shoot.

Student 1: The relationship with my parents. They've known me since I was born. Actually, probably before I was born. They tell me that they used to play Mozart for me when my mom was still pregnant and I would start kicking.

Student 2: Right. And the relationship with *my* mother will be especially long, because I know she'll never stop mothering me.

Student 3: Well... I think maybe my longest relationship will be with my own kids.

Student 4: No, no. It's got to be with your spouse, because you'll know him before your kids.

Student 5: Actually, I'm not sure I'll ever get married, so maybe my longest relationship will be with my dog.

Professor: Well, these are all reasonable assumptions, and they may turn out to be true for some of you, (and I hope that Joe's dog sets a record for canine longevity)... but statistically, you have missed the mark, because, in fact, in most cases, the longest relationships any of us will have are with our siblings. Yes, that's right. Think about it. Nobody else in our lives may know us "from beginning to end." In the U. S., about 80 percent of us have at least one sibling and you typically know your siblings from the day you (or they) are born. Certainly this is sooner than you will know your spouses or children. And, generally, you and your siblings can expect to live longer than your parents and certainly a lot longer than the average dog.

OK... So today we're going to talk about sibling relationships... some of the key issues that affect their development within the family... and how these relationships affect your social development outside the family through your entire life.

Students: Wow. I never thought about it like that. Sure. Sounds good.

Professor: OK. First off, let me ask what you believe, what assumptions you make, based on your own experience or observations, about siblings. Just raise your hands if you agree with the following statements:

1. By and large, siblings who grow up under the same roof will have similar impressions or memories about family interactions. OK, I see that about 75 percent of you agree with this statement. Next statement...

2. Even though you may feel that your parents have a favorite child, parents really do love their children equally and seldom play favorites. Ah, yes. I hear a little nervous laughter here and

fewer hands went up, but we still have about 55–60 percent of you who agree with this statement. That still leaves quite a few of you who may suffer from what I like to call the "Mom always liked you best" syndrome. I'm curious though. How many of you are parents of two or more children? OK... now how many of *you* agree that you love your children equally? OK... just as I thought. About 95 percent of these parents agree that no matter how their children may feel, they really *do* love their children equally. Next statement...

3. For the most part, it's much better for a child to grow up in a home where there is no fighting or competition with siblings. Hmm. Some of you look surprised that about 90 percent of you raised your hands. We'll touch later on why you felt that you might be the only one to feel that way. And the last statement...

4. If, in fact, it *is* true that your parents actually *do* tend to "play favorites," in general it would be best for your overall social development to actually be the favorite child rather than to be a less favored child. Ah, right. I see that you're thinking hard about this one. OK... now you must choose. Raise your hand if you agree. Let's see... 38, 39... That's a little over 75 percent of you who agree.

All right. Now let's look at these four assumptions one by one and see if researchers agree with you or if their findings will bust some myths, that is, alter your beliefs or assumptions, about siblings.

The first assumption, that siblings growing up in the same household will have similar impressions or memories of the same events or experiences is, more often than not... false. Congratulations to the 25 percent of you that remembered what you learned in Psychology 101 about the powers of observation and memory and the crucial role that emotions play in creating the size and shape of the window through which we observe and experience something. Do you remember the classic experiment of simulating a crime in front of a classroom of students and then asking them to describe what happened? Not only were most of the students not able to accurately remember what had actually happened, but almost none of them agreed with any of the other students about what had happened.

Student 1: I'm not surprised about that. I guess I just didn't think of sibling experiences in the family as being such a big deal.

Professor: Really? Judy Dunn, a British developmental psychologist says that a sibling relationship, being the first and often most important peer relationship an individual experiences, tends to be so highly emotionally charged that it can turn family life into a daily drama for children, each of whom is competing for a starring role.

Which brings us to the second assumption... that regardless of their children's perceptions, parents typically do love their children equally. Well, guess what everyone? Researchers have shown in several different studies that at least 65 percent of mothers and 70 percent of fathers exhibit a preference for one particular child. And the emphasis here is on *exhibit*. Many researchers now think that the other 30–35 percent just hide their preferences well from observers and even from themselves.

Student 2: I'm not sure this would be true in my culture. My parents play favorites sometimes and we all accept it and are happy with this.

Professor: Yes, of course. I understand this. Heidi Riggio, at California State University explains that not only is it painful for American parents to think about how they may have failed their children, whose experiences of favoritism, unfairness, even generally getting less love, are forever incorporated into their personalities, but also that while in other cultures parents may be willing to admit they treated the eldest son best, for example, this is not generally true in America, with its emphasis on fairness and equality. Dunn has also found that children who feel that they are being treated very differently than their siblings, can have serious difficulties in relationships for their entire lives. In addition, according to Clare Stocker at the University of Denver, they are at higher risk of developing anxiety, depression, and low self-esteem. And there are many famous folks from Freud to Dickens to Madonna who are examples of suffering the consequences of "least favored" status in the family.

So... what do you think now about assumption three? Is it better to grow up without competing or fighting with your siblings? Maybe more of you want to say "yes" now, but wait! Many family therapists claim that sibling rivalry, or competition, is normally a good thing. Family therapist Diane Barth claims that when siblings learn to fight and then negotiate a peace, they are learning a formula for resolving conflicts for the rest of their lives. On the other hand, if siblings hardly ever fight, then the opportunity to develop this skill may be lost. Psychologist Hara Marano suggests that the longevity of our relationships with our siblings leads to a deep sense of a shared fate and that we tend to replicate our sibling relationships in both work and in love.

So... on to the fourth assumption, that if we accept the fact that parents *do* play favorites, it is, generally speaking, best to be the favorite child in the family. I'm sure that by now you've caught on to the pattern here and know that I'm about to bust another myth. Jeffrey Kluger, in an article in *Time* magazine, tells us that, and I quote, "It would seem that being the favorite may boost self-esteem and confidence, but studies show it can also leave kids with a sense of arrogance and entitlement." Not very pleasant characteristics, right? He goes on to say that "Unfavored children may grow up wondering if they're somehow unworthy of the love the parents lavished on the golden child. But they [the unfavored children] may do better at forging relationships outside the family as a result of that."

Why do you think this is so? What do you think Kluger is getting at here? For homework, please read the Kluger article and then write a paragraph explaining what you think he means by this and then write another paragraph or two based on your own experience or observations either agreeing or disagreeing with Kluger.

OK? See you all next week. Have a great weekend.

See Part 2 Understanding Straw Man Arguments on page 186 of this audioscript.

Speaker 1

Mother: OK kids, here's the deal. I know that normally we divide up the household chores equally amongst you, but this week, your brother David has an important football game and he has to go to an extra practice and then he has to rest before the game. So Alan and Ruth, you're both going to have to pitch in more than usual to help me out if you want to go to the game on Friday night with your dad and me.

Question: What is the speaker's main point?

Speaker 2

Man: Honey, I don't know what's going on with Henry these days. He hardly ever calls us and when he does, all he does is complain about how we treat him. Then he wonders why we don't come over to visit with him and his children as often as we go to see his sisters and brothers and their kids. I really don't get it, do you? Besides, why would we want to visit him if he's just going to whine like a child about us playing favorites?

Question: What is the man trying to say to his wife?

Man: Sorry I'm late. I just finished a really difficult phone call and I needed a few minutes to figure out what to do about it.

Woman: Really? If you don't mind saying... What happened? Maybe I can help.

Man: No, no, it's OK. My dad just told me that they aren't going to be coming to visit us on their vacations anymore... that he and my Mom are going to my brother's house from now on and if we wanted to see them, that we'd have to go there.

Woman: Are you upset about that?

Man: No, I'm OK with that.

Woman: Well, you've told me how much you argue with him when he comes to your house, so maybe it's for the best, right?

Man: Sorry?

Woman: I mean, if he's so difficult, then let your brother deal with him.

Man: Wait a minute. That's a little cold. This is my dad we're talking about. I love the guy no matter what.

Woman: Why? You're always saying how much he always favored your brother over you when you were little.

Man: But that was a long time ago and it wasn't really his fault.

Woman: Right. We all know that your brother was sick a lot and needed extra attention. But missing your music concert? Come on! He could have found the time.

Man: Why are you being so tough on him? It was only one concert.

Woman: But it really hurt your feelings. So... if he feels more comfortable at your brother's house... just let him go there and forget about it.

Man: Well... I don't know. Maybe he won't be so comfortable being at my brother's. I know he's told me that my brother spoils his kids and that it's difficult to be around them sometimes because they have this sense of entitlement and are not respectful of him as their grandfather.

Woman: Still, if he came to your house, you'd just whine about him loving your brother best and then he wouldn't feel comfortable at your house either, right?

Man: OK, OK. I get it.

Woman: So you don't really believe that his decision is for the best, do you?

Man: Well, to be honest, not really. I think I'm going to call him back and try to smooth things over.

Woman: Good idea.

1. *Listen again to part of the conversation.*

Man: Sorry I'm late. I just finished a really difficult phone call and I needed a few minutes to figure out what to do about it.

Woman: Really? If you don't mind saying... What happened? Maybe I can help.

Man: No, no, it's OK. My dad just told me that they aren't going to be coming to visit us on their vacations anymore...

Question 1: What does the man mean by saying, "No, no, it's OK"?

Question 2: Why does the man mention the phone call?

3. *Listen again to part of the conversation.*

Woman: Are you upset about that?

Man: No, I'm OK with that.

Woman: Well, you've told me how much you argue with him when he comes to your house, so maybe it's for the best, right?

Man: Sorry?

Woman: I mean, if he's so difficult, then let your brother deal with him.

Man: Wait a minute. That's a little cold. This is my dad we're talking about. I love the guy no matter what.

Question 3: Why does the man think the woman is cold?

4. *Listen again to part of the conversation.*

Woman: Why? You're always saying how much he always favored your brother over you when you were little.

Man: But that was a long time ago and it wasn't really his fault.

Woman: Right. We all know that your brother was sick a lot and needed extra attention. But missing your music concert? Come on! He could have found the time.

Man: Why are you being so tough on him? It was only one concert.

Woman: But it really hurt your feelings. So... if he feels more comfortable at your brother's house... just let him go there and forget about it.

Question 4: Why does the woman mention the music concert?

Question 5: Why did the woman use straw man arguments throughout the conversation?

PART 2 Understanding and Using Analogies

2 Listening for the "Gist" or Main Ideas page 65

3 Listening for Analogies page 65

Study Session Conversation:
What Makes Us Tick—The Cardiac Muscle

Ali: So, what are we studying next, Greta?

Greta: Let's go over the notes from Professor Miller's lecture, Ali.

Ali: You mean the lecture on the heart?

Greta: Uh-huh.

Fred: Great idea. Why don't we go through the notes and make sure we understand everything?

Greta: Sure, Fred.

Ali: OK. Let me just get my notes out. All right. Ready.

Greta: Well, first she said it was the action of the cardiac muscles that makes an organ as small as the heart so incredibly efficient. And then she talked about how the shape of the heart is similar to a pear. I don't exactly understand that analogy. I mean, which way is the pear supposed to be leaning?

Fred: Well, think of the pictures Professor Miller showed us. In my opinion, it *did* look like a pear, right side up, with the widest part at the bottom, leaning a little to the right.

Greta: Yeah, I get it now. OK, let's talk about the parts. It's got four hollow chambers—two in the top part and two in the bottom part. And what did she say about the walls of the heart?

Fred: She said that they're fairly thick, approximately like a slice of bread, at the bottom. You may not agree with me, but I don't think that's a great analogy. It depends on what kind of bread you have in mind, right? But what she said about the top of the heart makes more sense to me. She said that at the top, they're thinner, about as thin as an orange peel.

Greta: Are you sure about that? I'm fairly certain that it was the other way around.

Ali: No, I'm positive Fred is right. I have it right here in my notes.

Greta: OK. Now what else? Oh, yeah… The strips of muscle at the bottom of the heart are like string around a hollow ball. How's that for an analogy?

Fred: That's good.

Greta: You know, I was surprised that the heart is so small. It's only slightly larger than a tightly closed fist. I like how Professor Miller had us each make a fist and look at it so we could see that it was about the same size as a heart.

Ali: Then remember how she told us to open and close our hands? She wanted us to see how the muscles contract and relax over and over again our whole lives.

Fred: Yup. That's the heartbeat. Contraction and relaxation—very regular and even—the beat is just like the tick-tock of a clock.

Greta: But didn't she say that the rate can vary?

Fred: Yeah… In general, the rate of the heartbeat varies in relation to the size of the person or animal. An elephant's heart rate is about 30 beats per minute. A small bird's heart rate is about 1,000 beats per minute. The heart of a human infant at birth beats about 130 times a minute. In a small child, it beats about 90 to 100 times a minute. The average adult rate for men is about 75 beats per minute. And the rate for a woman averages about seven to eight beats faster per minute than the rate for men. Why is that?

Ali: I think she said that's because women are smaller than men, but I don't really understand why that is. Do you, guys?

Fred: No, not really.

Greta: Let's ask her in class.

Ali: OK. Hmm… Anyway, I think it's pretty amazing that this adds up to about 100,000 heartbeats a day for an adult male. That's about 2,600,000,000 heartbeats in a lifetime.

Fred and Greta: Wow!

Ali: Yeah, and another amazing thing is that the heart doesn't have any nerves in it. So, no messages are sent from the brain through the nerves to the cardiac muscles. The brain doesn't tell the cardiac muscles to beat. Nothing does.

Fred: So that means that the heartbeat starts in the cardiac muscle itself?

Greta: That's right. It's different from the other muscles and organs in that way.

Fred: Oh, yeah. Remember what Professor Miller said about how a very small piece of cardiac muscle can be kept alive in a dish with a special liquid in it? And that the muscle will continue to beat all by itself!

Ali: Uh-huh. Scientists don't really understand how the cardiac muscle does this yet, but I bet they will in ten or fifteen years.

Fred: OK, but how does the heart work with all of the other organs?

Ali: Well, the heart is similar to a pump. Basically, it pumps blood to the rest of the body. Let's see, I've got it here in my notes. The heart pumps approximately five quarts of blood a minute if you are resting and thirty-five quarts of blood a minute if you are exercising hard. For light activity, the heart pumps 4,500 gallons a day. If you lived until you were eight years old and just slept all the time, your heart would still pump about 52,560,000 gallons—or 198,961,244 liters—of blood in a lifetime! Can you believe that the heart works that hard?

Fred: Don't look so worried, Ali. I'm pretty sure your heart isn't going to quit yet.

Greta: Right. Remember… Professor Miller said that the heart rests a lot, too. In fact, a heartbeat takes eight-tenths of a second, and half of that time the heart rests. So it's both hard-working *and* efficient.

Fred: Yeah—I'd say you're going to be around for a good long time!

PART 3 Expressing Opinions

1 Recognizing a Know-It-All page 69

Conversation 1

Kenji: I suspect that heart disease is now the number one killer in the United States.

Paul: No, no! It's cancer.

Kenji: Well, I'm almost positive that it's got to be heart disease by now. Didn't Dr. Strong suggest last year that heart disease would soon overtake cancer as the number one…

Paul: Nope. You're wrong. That couldn't have happened yet. It's still cancer.

Conversation 2

Kenji: I suspect that heart disease is now the number one killer in the United States.

Paul: Oh, I always thought it was cancer.

Kenji: Well, I'm almost positive that it's got to be heart disease by now. Didn't Dr. Strong suggest last year that heart disease would soon overtake cancer as the number one killer?

Paul: Yes, she did, and I know that not everyone will agree with me, but I'm pretty sure that Dr. Strong hasn't read the latest statistics on this.

2 Listening for Personal Opinions page 69

See Part 2 Understanding and Using Analogies on page 190 of this audioscript.

PART 4 Focus on Testing

1 Pragmatic Understanding of Opinions: Brief Informal Speeches page 72

Speaker 1

Man: Personally, I don't think that anyone should smoke and I'm positive that smoking causes cancer. Of course, not everyone will agree with me, but I don't think we should make laws about what people can and can't do in restaurants and bars.

Question: What is the speaker implying?

Speaker 2

Woman: I should lose some weight. I read in the newspaper that most Americans are eight to sixteen pounds overweight, and I'm pretty sure that I'm part of this majority.

Question: What does the speaker think?

2 Expressing Opinions page 72

See Part 2 Understanding and Using Analogies on page 190 of this audioscript.

Question 1: Fred agrees with Professor in some ways and disagrees in others in regards to what the heart looks like. Explain what each person thinks and then give your own opinion about the appearance of the heart.

Question 2: What do the students agree to do to clarify a point they didn't understand from the lecture? Do you think this is the best way to handle this or do you have a better suggestion?

Question 3: What does Ali think scientists will be able to tell us about the heart in the future? Do you think this is realistic? Why or why not?

Question 4: What does Fred tease Ali about? Do you think that this is proper behavior among friends? Why or why not?

CHAPTER 5 High Tech, Low Tech

PART 2 Taking Notes on a Field Trip

3 Taking Notes page 80

4 Listening for Measurements and Amounts page 81

Field Trip: Spaceflight—A Simulation

Guide: Hello. We'd like to welcome Professor Chapman and his aeronautics class to Houston, Texas, and the Space Center. Today, without leaving the ground, we are going to experience the excitement of a flight into space.

We are now seated in the space center's amphitheater. The screen in front of you shows the inside of the space orbiter. The advanced technology used in this presentation will simulate for you what it is like to be a crew member at work on an actual space mission. Our mission today is to capture and repair a $75 million dollar solar observation satellite that has been in orbit since 1980.

OK. Fasten your seatbelts and we will begin our simulated flight on the spaceship *Enterprise*.

All right? Now, imagine we have been inside the orbiter for about two hours making sure everything is ready.

Mission Control: This is Mission Control. It is now T minus 3.8 seconds.

Guide: T stands for takeoff, of course. And we hear the three engines fire.

Mission Control: T minus one second. T minus zero.

Guide: At T minus zero, the two booster rockets fire, and three seconds later we are lifted off the ground by the combined energy of the five engines.

Through the window we see the tower disappear. We feel the effects of acceleration on our bodies as our spaceship speeds up to four times the speed of sound (which is about 1,100 feet per second in the air) and revolves 120 degrees. We are now turned upside down with our heads toward the ground as we climb in the air and go out over the ocean. How do you like the feeling? We won't be right side up until we are in orbit.

Two minutes after takeoff, the fuel in the booster rockets has been used up. They drop away as we continue gaining speed. Six minutes later we have reached fifteen times the speed of sound and the graceful spaceship is flying free, heading into orbit around Earth at a height of 690 miles.

Once we reach full altitude we change our program on the computer. This shuts down the main engines and the external tank drops away. We can now control the orbiter's movement with small bursts of rocket fire from engines in the nose and tail. Put your hand on the control stick. Move the control stick to the right and we'll roll. Although we don't feel it without gravity, you can see the motion through the window. If you move your wrist on the control forward or backward, we will go up or down. A twist makes us go to the right or left.

Let's have a few of you take turns with this, so you can get the full effect.

Student 1: My turn? OK. Here we go. Lean left!

Student 2: OK, now I'll straighten us up.

Student 3: Anyone for a complete roll?

All Students: Enough! Enough! I'm getting dizzy!

Guide: OK. Let's get ready for the next phase of your mission. Look through the window. The cargo doors are opening. These doors open when we arrive in orbit and remain open to provide the ship with necessary ventilation throughout our stay in space. As I said before, the purpose of this mission is to repair a $75 million dollar solar observation satellite that has been in orbit since 1980. Since the failure of its control system, the satellite has been moving through space without guidance—moving so fast that it cannot be reached directly by the Remote Manipulation Arm, which we'll call the RMA.

The RMA is a fifty-foot mechanical arm attached to the outside of the orbiter. Look at the handout we gave you as you came into the amphitheater. From the drawing, you can see that the mechanical arm is very much like your own arm. The arm is attached to the orbiter at the shoulder, and an elbow and a wrist allow the arm to move and bring satellites into the cargo bay. This maneuver is necessary in order to repair the satellite. There are television cameras at both the elbow and wrist so we can see what's going on. The hand, or what is called the *end effector*, is fitted with three inside wires. A short arm of the satellite is caught by these wires.

If you look out the window, you will see two astronauts in space suits outside. They are going to slow down the satellite manually so we can connect it to the RMA from here inside. Remember, we said that the satellite was moving too quickly to be picked up directly by the RMA.

Student 1: Wow! Look at that!

Student 2: Yeah, they're actually grabbing the satellite with their hands!

Guide: Now it's our turn. The astronauts outside have captured the satellite for us and now we have to get to work. We must manipulate the arm, bending its wrist, elbow, and shoulder joints to lower the damaged satellite into our cargo bay.

Great job! OK, now let's wait while the astronauts repair the satellite in the cargo bay. It should only take a few moments. Just a small part on the outside of it needs to be replaced. Uh-huh, they almost have the old part off. That's it. Now they're putting the new part in place. And tightening it down. There! I think they've got it!

Mission Control: *Enterprise*, this is Mission Control. Congratulations! Your mission has been accomplished. Now prepare for reentry.

Guide: OK, crew, let's get ready for reentry by closing the cargo bay doors. We fire our engines to slow the orbiter so that it begins to fall toward Earth. We enter the atmosphere at an altitude of 400,000 feet. We are now 5,000 miles from our landing site. The friction of air causes us to slow down from our entry speed of 16,000 miles per hour, but it also causes us to heat up. However, we are protected from surface temperatures of 2,750 degrees Fahrenheit by the thermal tiles covering the ship. The heat is so great that our radio communications are cut off for twelve minutes on our descent. Our onboard computers maintain control.

As the atmosphere gets heavier, our craft changes from a spaceship into a glider. The engines shut off as we continue our descent in silence. The ground is coming up at us fast at 10,000 feet per minute, seven times faster than it would in the landing of an airplane. At just 1,500 feet our stomachs feel funny as the pilot pulls up the nose of the spaceship to slow us down. We hear the landing gear open and lock, and very quickly, we touch back down on Mother Earth and come to a stop.

The flight is over. Mission accomplished! Thanks for coming aboard the *Enterprise*.

PART 3 Shifting Between Active and Passive Voice

1 Contrasting the Active and Passive Voice page 84

Conversation 1

Astronaut 1: Wow! Did you see how much damage was caused by that hurricane when you drove through town?

Astronaut 2: Yeah, the launch pad was hit, too. Mission Control says that the orbiter liftoff for today has been canceled until further notice and they'll let us know as soon as it's been rescheduled.

Conversation 2

Astronaut 1: I'm really worried about that hurricane. It certainly could cause a serious delay for the launch today.

Astronaut 2: Right. I don't mind the delays so much when we can wait at home, or even on the base. But once we get into our gear and board, I really dread any delays.

Astronaut 1: Yeah, me too. I once sat all suited up for eight and a half hours... waiting for a big storm to pass.

Conversation 3

Engineer: Hi, Kim. Can you check out a small problem for me?

Supervisor: Sure. Oh, why is that warning light flashing?

Engineer: I think something strange happened on the lift off.

Supervisor: Look there. Can you see that black spot?

Engineer: Oh, no! Some insulation foam must have broken off and damaged the shuttle!

Conversation 4

Supervisor: Hello, and welcome to the Space Center.

Reporter: Hello. Murat Boonto from the *International Times*. Is there going to be a problem bringing the astronauts home safely?

Supervisor: Just a small one. It seems that a small piece of insulation foam was damaged during liftoff.

Reporter: What? Was the shuttle damaged, too?

Supervisor: Yes. A protective tile was hit by the foam and we can now see a large black spot on the tile.

Conversation 5

Husband: What happened?

Wife: The lights just went out!

Husband: What do you suppose is the reason?

Wife: Maybe aliens have landed in a spacecraft on our front lawn. But more likely… the electric company probably turned off our electricity because we forgot to pay our bill when we were on vacation.

Conversation 6

Electric company official: Good morning. This is Madison Electric.

Customer: My name is Ellie Barca and my electricity went out last night.

Electric company official: Just a minute, Ms. Barca. I'll check you records.

Customer: Thank you.

Electric company official: Ah, yes, here they are.

Customer: What happened?

Electric company official: Your electricity has been turned off because your bill hasn't been paid.

Customer: Well… good. We can take care of that. At least it's not because we've been attacked by aliens.

2 Listening for the Passive Voice
page 85

See Part 2 Taking Notes on a Field Trip on page 192 of this audioscript.

PART 4 Focus on Testing

1 Note-Taking Practice page 87

Guide: OK, everyone. Welcome to the Thompson University Science Museum. Thanks for coming today to see our new exhibit, "Low-Tech Solutions." This exhibit is a slightly humorous look at how clever people have found simple solutions to complicated problems.

Student 1: You mean, like, fixing things with chewing gum and hair pins?

Guide: You're not too far off, as you'll see. Our first exhibit features the mighty, the versatile

aluminum foil. As famous as foil is for replacing pot covers or cookie sheets, it also fixes cars, satellite dishes, and even computer keyboards. Look at this dirty and rusted-out car muffler, which is the part that keeps cars from running too noisily. Next to it, you see a similar muffler wrapped in three layers of ordinary aluminum foil, kept in place by two "ropes" made of speaker wire from a sound system.

Student 2: Cool. But does it work?

Guide: Listen to this. First, I'll play a recording of a car running with a brand-new muffler. Now I'll press this button, and we can hear the car running with the falling-apart muffler. Finally, let's hear the repaired muffler. There. So what do we learn from this?

Student 2: Keep foil in your car.

Guide: Anything else?

Student 3: Yeah. You can save a lot of money if you're smart. A new muffler would have been expensive.

Guide: Right! OK, let's move on. What do you see in this display case?

Student 2: A horn.

Student 1: A clarinet.

Guide: Right. A clarinet. A broken clarinet. Now, this is a finely crafted instrument, made by artistic masters and tested by some very sophisticated machines. So what's wrong with it?

Student 3: You can see from that blow-up photo. One of those hole covers looks thinner or harder or something.

Guide: Right. It looks harder because it has lost a little soft piece that normally goes on the end of the key. That soft cover, called a *pad*, makes sure that the tone hole is completely covered when the key is at rest. So, you're a clarinetist just about to go on stage, and one of those pads falls off. What do you do? Rush off to an instrument repair shop?

Student 1: No. You fix it yourself.

Guide: How?

Student 1: Uh, I'm not sure.

Guide: Well, here's how the Thompson Orchestra's first clarinetist fixed it. She pulled some chewing gum out of her purse and gave it a few chews. Then she picked up the fallen pad and used the gum to glue it to the end of the key. She got through her performance without any trouble.

Student 3: Pretty clever of her. I had given up chewing gum, but I think I'll start again.

Guide: Well, you'll have to discuss that with your dentist. Now, before we move on, let me ask you something. You're trying to get a DVD out of a DVD player. You know it's in there, but it won't come out because the tray keeps getting stuck. You could take it to a repair shop and pay $40 to have it removed, but what do you really do?

Student 2: I don't know. Shake the player? Pry it out with a butter knife?

Guide: Let's forget about the butter knife method... unless you want a jolt of electricity through your body, but shaking sometimes works. Look here. That's what our next display is about.

1. Listen again to part of the exchange.

Guide: OK, everyone. Welcome to the Thompson University Science Museum. Thanks for coming today to see our new exhibit, "Low-Tech Solutions." This exhibit is a slightly humorous look at how clever people have found simple solutions to complicated problems.

Question 1: Which of the following does the tour guide most strongly imply about low-tech solutions?

Question 2: According to the tour guide, what item in the exhibit was fixed by using aluminum foil?

3. Listen again to part of the exchange.

Guide: Right. It looks harder because it has lost a little soft piece that normally goes on the end of the key. That soft cover, called a *pad*, makes sure that the tone hole is completely covered when the key is at rest. So, you're a clarinetist just about to go on stage, and one of those pads falls off. What do you do? Rush off to an instrument repair shop?

Student 1: No. You fix it yourself.

Guide: How?

Student 1: Uh, I'm not sure.

Guide: Well, here's how the Thompson Orchestra's first clarinetist fixed it. She pulled some chewing gum out of her purse and gave it a few chews. Then she picked up the fallen pad and used the gum to glue it to the end of the key. She got through her performance without any trouble.

Question 3: Why, according to the tour guide, was the solution involving gum especially helpful for the clarinetist?

4. Listen again to part of the exchange.

Guide: Well, you'll have to discuss that with your dentist. Now, before we move on, let me ask you something. You're trying to get a DVD out of a DVD player. You know it's in there, but it won't come out because the tray keeps getting stuck. You could take it to a repair shop and pay $40 to have it removed, but what do you really do?

Student 2: I don't know. Shake the player? Pry it out with a butter knife?

Guide: Let's forget about the butter knife method... unless you want a jolt of electricity through your body, but shaking sometimes works. Look here. That's what our next display is about.

Question 4: Which of the following is most likely to come next in the tour?

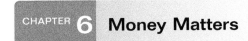

CHAPTER 6 **Money Matters**

PART 2 Understanding and Constructing Pro and Con Arguments

3 **Listening for Pros and Cons** page 97

Radio Program: The World Bank Under Fire

Michelle Barney: Good afternoon. This is Radio K-I-Z-Z, your "total talk" radio station. I am Michelle Barney, financial reporter for Radio KIZZ, and I will be your host for today's program, "The World Bank Under Fire."

I'm sure you are all aware that most of the world's population lives in developing and semi-industrialized countries. These countries do not have enough money to invest in schools, utilities, factories, and highways. One way these countries can get money is by borrowing money from an organization called the World Bank.

In theory, this money should be helping the world's poor. Since the establishment of the World Bank in 1944, most people have assumed that these loans could only do good things for a country. But it turns out that money isn't everything.

For example, many people question the value of a dam built with World Bank money in Ethiopia. That dam was built to provide electricity, but it destroyed the homes and lives of more people than it served with electric power. That dam also destroyed forests and endangered animals and plants. The critics of the World Bank say that this kind of help to developing countries is wasteful, destructive, and unfair. They wonder who is profiting from projects such as this one—the people or large international corporations.

Today we have a spokesperson here with us from the World Bank, Mr. George Cruz. Mr. Cruz has been with the Bank for ten years and is part of a team that has been examining the effectiveness of World Bank projects. This World Bank team of insiders is coming to the same conclusions as many critics of the World Bank. They have concluded that many of the projects in the past have been economic failures and serious threats to both the environment and human rights. Mr. Cruz…

George Cruz: Well, Ms. Barney, I am very happy to be here today to clarify some things about the World Bank. While much of what you say is true, I think we need to talk about the successes of the World Bank as well as the failures. We also need to talk about the positive changes the World Bank has made in its policies and goals for the 21st century.

But to begin, I'd like to give a brief overview of the World Bank and how it works.

Ms. Barney: Of course. I think that would be very helpful for our listeners.

Mr. Cruz: Now, what we call the World Bank is actually an umbrella term, a general term, for five separate organizations with five slightly different purposes. But the International Bank for Reconstruction and Development is generally what most people think of as the World Bank. In order to borrow money from this branch of the World Bank, a country must be a member. Of course, the money is supposed to be paid back with interest, as with any bank loan.

Ms. Barney: Yes. I guess that's true, but many countries are never able to pay back the loans.

Mr. Cruz: Yes, that has been a serious problem, but we do have a program to restructure the loans, which will alleviate that problem.

Ms. Barney: Yes, restructuring, or reorganizing how the debts are paid back, may help a little. But unless they are forgiven completely so that nothing has to be paid back, there are still very serious problems. Isn't it true that in some cases, developing countries have been forced to cut spending on health, education, transportation, and welfare programs in order to reduce their huge debts to the World Bank? I've read that in some countries, the debt to the World Bank is so great that it's now the largest item in the government budgets. Furthermore, these countries have been forced to sell industries and land to foreign corporations in order to pay off debts to the World Bank.

Mr. Cruz: Wait, wait! One thing at a time! First, you're right that developing countries owe a lot of money to the World Bank. However, as of this year, twenty-two nations have had at least two-thirds of their debts forgiven. They don't have to make any more payments. And, don't forget, there is a danger that if a debt is forgiven completely, that it will ruin that nation's credit rating, because everyone will think that country just doesn't know how to manage money and pay its bills. So we have to be concerned about this, too.

Ms. Barney: I see.

Mr. Cruz: And I hope everyone understands the International Bank for Reconstruction and Development tries to loan money to member countries for projects that will aid economic development. In theory, this is good. But up to now, the bank could only loan money to buy imported goods. And to make sure that this rule was followed, the bank paid the sellers directly.

Ms. Barney: Well, this rule is good for the countries and companies that want to sell goods to developing countries, but wouldn't this discourage local production of goods? In the long term, wouldn't this rule do more harm than good to the developing country's economy?

Mr. Cruz: Possibly. That's one of the things we're looking at very seriously. But there are other advantages to getting a loan from this branch of the World Bank. The International Bank for Reconstruction and Development provides technical assistance along with loans. And this is a major part of our new vision for the 21st century.

For example, Cameroon submitted a proposal for a new irrigation system along the Logone River. They hoped that with this new irrigation system, the cash income of the region would be five times greater than before. But the Bank did not approve the project right away because we know that technological advances can sometimes cause environmental problems. Before approving the proposal, the Bank asked environmental consultants to study the project.

The consultants found that the new irrigation system would result in a serious health problem because of snails that live in the area. These snails carry a tropical disease called bilharzia.

Ms. Barney: Excuse me. Was that bilharzia with an *h*?

Mr. Cruz: Yes. Bil-har-zee-uh. Bilharzia. Anyway, the new irrigation system might have spread the snails and the disease they carried to a larger area. So the Bank paid for studies of the river system. Scientists and engineers together determined that if the irrigation system were used only when the snails were not breeding, then the disease would not spread. So, the Bank was able to solve the problem.

Ms. Barney: Yes, I understand what you mean, but wasn't there a problem getting local residents to use the system appropriately? I believe I read that some people were never convinced that the snail disease had really been taken care of, so they would not use the irrigation system at all. And another group of people never believed there was a problem in the first place, so they would not stop using the irrigation system when the snails were breeding.

Mr. Cruz: Yes, that's true. The International Bank for Reconstruction and Development is beginning to see that understanding local needs and culture may be more important than anything else in the success of a project.

Well, let me continue. The second organization under the World Bank umbrella is the International Development Association, or IDA. The IDA has approximately 160 members and makes loans that are interest free. This means that the borrowers do not have to pay any interest and they only pay back the loan amount, or principal. This, of course, is good because it allows even the poorest countries to begin projects immediately. On the other hand, because little or no interest is paid, the IDA is very dependent upon contributions from member nations to support various projects. The IDA uses the member dues, the yearly membership fees, plus other contributions from member nations, to fund loans to needy countries.

Ms. Barney: So, this is how member nations can dictate what governmental policies must be in place before loans will be given, right?

Mr. Cruz: Yes, exactly. The member nations, since they are contributing the money, often wish to have a say in how their money will be handled in a particular country. Some countries may be uncomfortable with the more powerful nations exerting this kind of control over their government policies. However, our major goal for the 21st century is to help people to help themselves, not only by providing money, but also by sharing knowledge and forming partnerships.

So, let's move on to the third organization in the World Bank group: the International Finance Corporation, or IFC. The IFC is different from the International Bank for Reconstruction and Development and the IDA because the IFC can invest in private business and industry, while the other two organizations can only invest in government projects. This is good for the country because the government does not have to guarantee the loan, and it encourages the growth of private business and industry. However, the IFC is not protected if the business fails. Also, the IFC has no control over how a company spends its money. Some people argue that the loan is more effective if people in the region spend the money in ways they think are best, without the IFC telling them what to do. They think that people outside the region do not have a thorough understanding of complex cultural and economic regional issues.

Ms. Barney: Absolutely, but is that ever really possible? I thought that the member nations get voting rights based on the amount of money they contribute to the Bank. Doesn't that mean that the wealthier nations have the most influence on which projects will be financed?

Mr. Cruz: Ideally, of course, the loans are made to countries on the basis of economic need alone. Robert McNamara, who was secretary of defense when John F. Kennedy was president of the United States, was president of the World Bank for a time. He hoped that the World Bank would be a model of international cooperation free from political self-interests. He hoped for a world in which the superpowers would join together to provide financial support for developing nations instead of arguing among themselves. But, we all know that it is difficult to separate economic goals from political interests in today's world.

Ms. Barney: I couldn't agree more with McNamara's vision. But whether the World Bank can really make this dream a reality is a big question. Well, our time is up and that brings us to the end of this week's program. Our guest today was George Cruz and the topic was "The World Bank Under Fire." Thank you for being with us today, Mr. Cruz.

Mr. Cruz: My pleasure.

Ms. Barney: This is Michelle Barney, your host for *World Business Topics*. Please join us next week, same time, same station, K-I-Z-Z, your "total talk" radio.

 Listening for Appropriate Uses of Expressions page 101

Conversation 1

Instructor: And furthermore, it is my opinion that if this small country had not received financial aid from friendly countries, the war would have been lost.

Student: You've got to be kidding! Military planning was the key.

Conversation 2

Instructor: And furthermore, it is my opinion that if this small country had not received financial aid from friendly countries, the war would have been lost.

Student: Yes, but isn't it also true that excellent military planning helped?

Conversation 3

Roger: Hey, Paul. Looks like we're having broccoli again! The only time we have anything decent to eat is when my parents visit! Then the food is so good that my parents don't understand why I think the food is overpriced.

Paul: Yes, Roger. That's precisely the point. They want to make parents think we eat well every day.

Conversation 4

Roger: Hey, Paul. Looks like we're having broccoli again! The only time we have anything decent to eat is when my parents visit! Then the food is so good that my parents don't understand why I think the food is overpriced.

Paul: You can say that again, Roger. They really do a good job of making parents think we eat that well every day.

Conversation 5

First board member: It's obvious that if we don't branch into other areas, eventually the company will fail.

Second board member: I don't believe that! We must cut costs!

Conversation 6

Third board member: It's obvious that if we don't branch into other areas, eventually the company will fail.

Fourth board member: That's more or less true; however, I think that by cutting our costs we can accomplish a great deal.

Conversation 7

Doctor: Mrs. Franklin, your son has a variety of medical problems related to his weight, and it's absolutely essential that he get more exercise.

Mrs. Franklin: You can say that again! He's too fat! All he does is watch TV and play video games!

Conversation 8

Doctor: Mrs. Franklin, your son has a variety of medical problems related to his weight, and it's absolutely essential that he get more exercise.

Mrs. Franklin: I couldn't agree with you more, Dr. Lewis. I've been trying to get him to play sports for years.

2 Agreeing and Disagreeing page 103

See Part 2 Understanding and Constructing Pro and Con Arguments on page 196 of this audioscript.

PART 4   Focus on Testing

1 Making Inferences: Brief Conversations page 106

Conversation 1

Woman: It's nice that banks are beginning to make more loans to people with low incomes. On the other hand, that money comes with a lot of strings attached.

Man: Yeah, I know what you mean.

Question: What is the woman implying?

Conversation 2

Man: You can say that again! I couldn't agree with you more. It's definitely better to pay cash than to pay interest for years and years.

Woman: Yes, but don't forget there are exceptions to that rule.

Question: What is the woman implying? (Choose two.)

2 Making Inferences: Radio Program page 106

1. *Listen to part of the radio program again.*

Ms. Barney: Since the establishment of the World Bank in 1944, most people have assumed that these loans could only do good things for a country. But it turns out that money isn't everything.

Question 1: What is the speaker implying?

2. *Listen to part of the radio program again.*

Ms. Barney: Today we have a spokesperson here with us from the World Bank, Mr. George Cruz. Mr. Cruz has been with the Bank for ten years and is part of a team that has been examining the effectiveness of World Bank projects.

Question 2: What is the speaker inferring about Mr. Cruz?

3. *Listen to part of the radio program again.*

George Cruz: Well, Ms. Barney, I am very happy to be here today to clarify some things about the World Bank. While much of what you say is true, I think we need to talk about the successes of the World Bank as well as the failures.

Question 3: What is Mr. Cruz inferring about Ms. Barney's attitude toward the World Bank?

4. *Listen to part of the radio program again.*

Mr. Cruz: The International Bank for Reconstruction and Development provides technical assistance along with loans. And this is a major part of our new vision for the 21st century.

Question 4: What is Mr. Cruz inferring about World Bank projects in the future?

Question 5: Overall, what do you think Mr. Cruz is implying about local needs and culture in relation to both past and future World Bank projects?

6. *Listen to part of the radio program again.*

Mr. Cruz: Robert McNamara, who was secretary of defense when John F. Kennedy was president of the United States, was president of the World Bank for a time. He hoped that the World Bank would be a model of international cooperation free from political self-interests. He hoped for a world in which the superpowers would join together to provide financial support for developing nations instead of arguing among themselves. But, we all know that it is difficult to separate economic goals from political interests in today's world.

Question 6: What is Mr. Cruz implying about the ideals of Robert McNamara?

CHAPTER 7 **Remarkable Individuals**

Celebrity Profile: Lance Armstrong, Uphill Racer

Joe Hemmings: Hello. This is Joe Hemmings, and I'm pleased to welcome you to "Celebrity Profile," the show that tells the stories of people in the news who have done remarkable things and lived remarkable lives. I just love the story we're going to tell you today, and I'm certain you will, too.

Lance Armstrong races bicycles. And he's pretty good at it. He's also a father. He's pretty good at that, too. This doesn't sound very special at first, but there is much more to Lance Armstrong's story. Armstrong's win in the 1999 Tour de France bicycle race is one of the most amazing stories in sports history. He was only the second American to win this race, and the win came after he had successfully battled a very deadly form of cancer.

This battle is where our profile begins. When Armstrong found out that he had cancer in October of 1996, his whole world fell apart. He couldn't bear the thought of never racing again, never marrying, and never having children. However, Armstrong says that it was his battle with cancer that transformed his body so he could become the best uphill racer in the world, and transformed his spirit so that he could become a better team member and a husband and father.

By 1996, when he was only 25, Armstrong had already become an international cycling champion. He was riding high on his fame, happy in his role as the wild, beer-drinking boy from Texas. He was young and undisciplined, and the sports writers called him "the Bull from Texas." He had come a long way from his small hometown of Plano, Texas. He was very poor when he left Plano in 1990, but by 1996, he was making over $1 million a year. At that time, though, he still had not won the most famous of all the races—the Tour de France.

In October of 1996, he was told that he had cancer and that he would have to endure treatments of chemotherapy to eliminate twelve tumors in his chest. Eventually, he would have surgery to remove a tumor that had also formed in his brain. Things did not look good. The doctors told him that he had only a fifty percent chance to live, and they did not even bother to discuss the future of his bicycle-racing career.

When he first began the chemotherapy treatments, he was able to keep up with his teammates on the training rides. Eventually, however, he began to ride more and more slowly. His teammates and friends couldn't stand to see him become depressed by this, so they also rode slowly. He therefore didn't realize just how poor his health had become until one day, a fifty-year-old woman on a heavy mountain bike passed him as he was struggling uphill on his superlight racing bike.

Most people thought that Armstrong would never race again, but he says that it was actually the chemotherapy that gave him the body he needed to win the Tour de France. He thinks that, due to the effects of chemotherapy, he was able to lose a lot of heavy muscle that he had built up from swimming as a teenager in Texas. This gave him the opportunity to rebuild his body from scratch, completely from the beginning. This time, he was careful during his training to build the kind of strong and light muscles needed to climb the mountain stages of the Tour de France. And by 1999, he was ready.

However, winning the Tour de France was not the highlight of that year for Armstrong. He and all of his fans were thrilled when his wife, Kristin, whom he had married a couple of years before, gave birth to their son, Luke, in the fall of 1999. And, a couple of years later in 2001, they had twin girls. What a super year *that* was! Armstrong says that facing death helped him learn what was most important in life and that training for his comeback helped him develop the qualities needed for better relationships with friends and family.

But this is not the end of this amazing story. In July of both 2000 and 2001, Armstrong proved that his win in 1999 was not a fluke by winning a second and third time. No one could deny that he was back at the top of his sport. But wait! There's more! Armstrong was asked to be on the 2000 U.S. Olympic team, and while he was training, he was hit on a country road by a hit-and-run driver who did not stop to help him. His wife found him two hours later lying in the road with a broken vertebra.

But this remarkable individual could not be stopped. He didn't have time for feeling sorry for himself, and he was back on his bicycle within a few days. He even managed to win a bronze medal at the Olympic Games.

As most of you know, Armstrong did not stop at only three Tour de France wins. I'm delighted to tell you that he went on to win again in 2002, 2003, 2004, and 2005, becoming the only person ever to win this race seven times—and all of the wins in consecutive years! How did he accomplish this remarkable feat? Armstrong has said about himself:

"A slow death is not for me. I don't do anything slowly, not even breathe. I want to die when I'm 100 years old, with an American flag on my back, and the star of Texas on my helmet, after screaming down a mountain on a bicycle at 75 miles per hour. I want to cross one last finish line as my wife and ten children applaud, and then I want to lie down in a field of those famous French sunflowers and gracefully die."

Yes, this would certainly be the perfect ending to a most remarkable life. Since he made this statement, however, Armstrong and his wife, Kristin, have divorced. He was dating singer Sheryl Crow in 2004 and 2005. And it was Sheryl Crow who was there cheering at the finish line in Paris when he won in 2004 and for the incredible seventh win in 2005. He retired from professional cycling in 2005, he says, to be able to spend more time sharing parenting responsibilities with his ex-wife and raising money for cancer research.

This is Joe Hemmings. Good night, and please join us next week for another edition of "Celebrity Profiles."

PART 3 ## Expressing Likes and Dislikes, Pleasure and Displeasure

1 ### Listening for Consequences of Expressions and Tone page 119

Conversation 1

Interviewer: I'm happy to say we have quite a few remarkable people working for our company.

Applicant: Now this is my idea of a job!

Interviewer: Ah… yes… well, we have one Nobel Prize winner in physics and one in chemistry, and they're looking for an assistant to help them organize their notes for a book that must be completed by next month.

Applicant: Oh, no. I can't stand that kind of pressure!

Interviewer: Oh?

Conversation 2

Interviewer: I'm happy to say we have quite a few remarkable people working for our company.

Applicant: That's wonderful! I would love the opportunity to work with them.

Interviewer: Well, we have one Nobel Prize winner in physics and one in chemistry, and they're looking for an assistant to help them organize their notes for a book that must be completed by next month, so you must work hard to keep them on schedule.

Applicant: Actually, I enjoy organizational tasks. I'm sure that I can help them finish on time!

Interviewer: Well, why don't we go and meet them and see what they think?

Conversation 3

Rafael: Hey, want to go to the concert with me on Saturday? There's an amazing cellist who has been playing since she was three years old!

Ana: Oh, no… I hate that kind of music.

Rafael: Oh, well, I thought you might like it.

Ana: No, I don't have time for that sort of thing.

Conversation 4

Rafael: Hi! How about going to see that new play at the experimental theater tonight? I really love the director, and they say that the lead actor is sure to win an award for her performance.

Joyce: Thanks, but I don't especially like that type of theater.

Rafael: Oh, sorry, I thought you would.

Joyce: No, I dislike it because I usually don't understand what's happening.

2 Listening for Expressions of Likes and Dislikes, Pleasure and Displeasure page 119

See Part 2 Listening for Chronological Order on page 201 of this audioscript.

PART 4 Focus on Testing

1 Expressing Preferences page 122

Question 1: Lance Armstrong surely prefers biking to any other sport. Other people prefer less strenuous sports. Which type of sport do you prefer? Why? You have 20 seconds to prepare your answer and 45 seconds to speak.

Question 2: Lance Armstrong would prefer to have many children rather than just one. How about you? Would you prefer to have many children or just one? Why? You have 20 seconds to prepare your answer and 45 seconds to speak.

Question 3: Some people who are injured stop exercising until they are healed. Others, such as Lance Armstrong, quickly resume their activities, even though it might slow their

recovery. Which way of dealing with injuries would you prefer? Why? You have 20 seconds to prepare your answer and 45 seconds to speak.

Question 4: Whom do you admire more, a person who becomes famous as an academic (a professor, a researcher, etc.) or a person who succeeds in business? Why? You have 20 seconds to prepare your answer and 45 seconds to speak.

Question 5: Some remarkably talented young people become professional athletes instead of going to college. Others finish their college education before turning professional. Which would you prefer for yourself if you had remarkable athletic talent? Why? You have 20 seconds to prepare your answer and 45 seconds to speak.

CHAPTER 8 Creativity

PART 2 Listening for Signal Words

2 Listening for Main Points About Drive and Creativity page 131

3 Listening for Signal Words page 132

Lecture: Drive and Creativity in the Workplace: The Mismatch Between What Science Knows and What Business Does

Part 1

Professor: Today we will continue our discussion of the creative process by taking up the topic of what things might inhibit creativity in the workplace. There's a great book on this topic by Daniel H. Pink, called *Drive*. Have any of you read it?

Students: Not yet, but I've been meaning to.
I've heard of it, I think.
Yeah. I bought it. It's been on the best seller list.
Oh yeah. But isn't it about motivation?

Professor: Yes, it is. In fact, the subtitle is: *The Surprising Truth about What Motivates Us.* Let me explain. Pink says that it is the misunderstanding of what actually motivates or drives us that inhibits creativity and productivity in the workplace.

I know that you were expecting me to pick up right where I left off last time, but I think that since most of you haven't read this book yet, let me go over what the plan is for today. I will outline some of Pink's theories for you first, OK?

Students: Great.

That'll be helpful.

Sure.

Of course.

Professor: OK. Then let's get going. First we'll consider some background information that Pink provides in his opening chapters. Traditionally in the workplace management has motivated people to work harder, faster—better—with a system of rewards and punishments that we commonly call carrots and sticks, right? Let me explain. We are driven forward like a donkey with the promise of a reward, a carrot. Generally, this reward is money, a salary. But it can be other things such as insurance benefits, retirement plans, vacation time or even a nicer refrigerator in the lunchroom. Now if we don't produce, if we don't work hard enough, if the donkey doesn't move, what happens? We are punished. We are not actually beaten with a stick like a donkey, but we can lose salary or other rewards.

Pink says that the carrot and stick model, which is based on extrinsic motivators, things that come from the outside, may work for certain kinds of repetitive tasks that do not require much creativity, but certainly does not work for the more creative problem-solving type of work on which our modern society now depends. Let me illustrate. Researchers in one study found that children who loved to draw would draw whenever they had the chance. When the researchers began to judge the drawings for the number and quality of the drawings and give rewards for the most and the best drawings, after a few days, the children drew less and less or stopped drawing altogether. In another study university students were given a series of puzzles to solve. On the first day, the students generally found the puzzles to be challenging and fun and kept solving the puzzles at a high rate. On

the second day they were divided into two groups. The first group just continued solving whatever puzzles they were given. The second group was paid for each puzzle successfully completed in a certain amount of time. On the third day all of the students were given more puzzles to solve. Now, according to the stick and carrot model, the group that was paid should have done better and completed more puzzles correctly, right? But the truth is that this is not what happened at all. And this is Pink's point, that sometimes the carrot and stick model of rewards and punishments in the workplace will produce just the opposite of what we want to happen. Let me repeat: using carrots and sticks to motivate people not only doesn't get them to work harder, or faster, or better; it may even cause them to do less and be less creative. Why does this happen? Let me go over what Pink calls the "seven deadly flaws" of carrots and sticks.

First, because carrots and sticks are extrinsic or external motivators, they can crush intrinsic or internal motivators, the thoughts and feelings we have about the task, such as doing something just for the love of doing it. Now I'm not saying that we should never get rewarded or paid for our work. We all need a fair salary and benefits in order to live. But beyond that, it is the task itself, the work itself that must be rewarding enough to keep us at it, to keep us going. And apparently, as with the children and their drawings and the university students and the puzzles, when we interfere with the creative process by introducing judgment and rewards, a person can become less interested in performing the task. And this is the second deadly flaw. Carrots and sticks can actually diminish or reduce performance rather than increase it. Furthermore, it can inhibit or even completely crush creativity, and this is the third flaw of the carrot and stick model.

Now the fourth deadly flaw of the carrot and stick model is that it can crowd out good behavior. Think about this. What if people decide that they like the reward and will only work for the reward? For example, if your son is a good boy and takes out the trash every day without being asked, but then you decide to reward him and pay him for doing this task, there's no going back. Believe me, he'll never take out the trash again for free. And if you try to make him, he'll never enjoy the task as much or do it as happily again.

Now the fifth deadly flaw is that carrots and sticks can encourage cheating, shortcuts, and unethical behavior. I don't think I have to explain this one. We've all seen it, from cheating on exams, to cheating in sports, to cheating in business, just to get to the goal or the reward. And the sixth flaw is that rewards can become addictive, so addictive that people may take risks to gain these rewards that they would not normally take.

And finally, the worst flaw of the carrot and stick model according to Pink is that it encourages short-term uncreative thinking or solutions to problems rather than more long-term creative solutions. The perfect example of this is the serious recession that hit the world economy in 2008 and 2009. Everyone was focused on short-term goals, the buyer who wanted a house, the mortgage broker who wanted a commission on the sale, the Wall Street stock trader who wanted a new commodity or stock to sell, the politician who cared only that the economy was in good shape in his or her reelection year. They *all* ignored the long-term effects of their actions on themselves and others. And despite what you'd like to believe about honor and ethics in the workplace, it was this kind of short-term thinking and greedy grabbing of the rewards that caused the economies of many nations to collapse.

Part 2

So, I cannot emphasize enough that carrots and sticks are soooo last century. Scientists can demonstrate this, but when it comes to drive and creativity, there's a huge gap between what science knows and what businesses actually do. And in order to close this gap, businesses need to change, to upgrade their operating systems, just as they would upgrade their computers, and not look back.

OK, I can see by your faces that you're definitely intrigued and maybe a little frustrated. You're beginning to understand why Pink thinks that the carrot and stick model has serious limitations, but you're wondering if we abandon that model, then what would the upgrade be, right?

Students: Right.
Exactly.
You bet.

Professor: All right. Let me outline what Pink thinks the upgrade should be. He says that the new model to increase motivation and creativity in the workplace should have three essential elements: One, autonomy, two, mastery, and three, purpose.

Now, autonomy is connected to the desire to direct our own lives. Simply put, if we choose to do a task, rather than are ordered to do a task, we will do it better and more creatively. Let me illustrate with this story. At a software company called Atlassian, one of the owners, Mike Cannon-Brookes, decided to give his programmers a day to work on any problem they wanted, even if it wasn't part of their regular job. This day gave birth to several ideas for new products and many ideas for repairs and patches on existing products, so Cannon-Brookes decided to make this practice a permanent part of the Atlassian culture. Now, once every three months, the engineers and programmers can work on any software problem they want. The day begins on a Thursday afternoon and by Friday afternoon they must show the results of their work to the rest of the company. These days at Atlassian are called FedEx days, because people have to deliver something overnight. And the truth is that on these FedEx days, they produce some of their best work and are happiest doing it.

And this takes us to the second essential element of Pink's business model upgrade, which is mastery. Let's consider just what that is. He doesn't just mean by mastery to become proficient at something. He's referring instead to the urge or the desire to make progress and get better at something in a way that is totally absorbing and takes your complete concentration. Let me explain by summarizing an interesting study for you. Researchers found that 11,000 industrial scientists and engineers working at companies in the United States found that the desire for intellectual challenge, that is, the urge to master something new and engaging, was the best predictor of productivity. And when we are engaged in something that is intellectually challenging and takes complete concentration, we've got what's called *flow*, and time almost seems to exist outside of us and the task we are absorbed in. This is similar to what happens when athletes or artists or musicians or writers are doing their best work. We've all experienced this from time to time, and the truth is we do not experience it nearly enough in the workplace.

Now, purpose, the third essential element of Pink's model, is the deep desire to do what we do for a purpose that is greater than ourselves. Now this may seem to contradict what I said about the "me, me, me," "out for yourself" attitude that seems to be encouraged by the carrot and stick model. But the real story is that if you provide an adequate salary and benefits for people to live comfortably, and provide sufficient opportunities for autonomy and mastery, then people will be free of the seven flaws of the carrot and stick and their deep desire to be part of something more important than just themselves can come out. Most people really *do* want to make a contribution to society. So, to review. In Pink's model, purpose maximization walks hand in hand with profit maximization. Business leaders are finding that that can recruit and maintain the best possible workforce by giving workers opportunities to work for a greater good, while in an environment that promotes autonomy and mastery.

Oh, my. I see our time is nearly up. Let's discuss this further next session, and to conclude I will summarize briefly what I've said today. In order to promote creativity in the workplace, we need to upgrade company operating systems. We need to stop telling those employees who do the tasks that require creativity that if you do X, then you will get Y. We need to change the corporate culture from the carrot and stick system of rewards and punishments to a system that will tap into people's basic needs to work in an environment that provides opportunities for autonomy, mastery, and purpose.

Well, that's all for today. Thank you, and see you next week.

PART 3   Divulging Information

1 Listening for Ways of Divulging Information page 138

Conversation 1

Antoine: Did you hear that Mr. Richards resigned from his post as president of the company?

Dashika: Yeah. I heard that story, too.

Antoine: Why do you say it's a story?

Dashika: Because I've heard what's really going on. The fact of the matter is that he was forced to quit—fired, in fact.

Antoine: No kidding? Why?

Dashika: Despite what you believe about him, he doesn't like these new FedEx days. He's pretty wedded to the old carrot and stick model and really thinks this new program to increase drive and creativity is a total waste of time.

Conversation 2

Katya: Hey, what gives? That's a really fine motorcycle Jesse is riding. Where'd he get the cash?

David: I don't know.

Katya: Oh, come on—what's the scoop?

David: Well, he says he won the money gambling in Las Vegas, but here's the real story. He entered a creativity competition that was advertised in the newspaper and he won.

Katya: I thought he told Penny that he couldn't stand those silly contests.

David: Well, despite what you may have heard, the real story is that he's been entering various contests about every other week and he finally won.

Katya: So, what's the big deal? Why doesn't he want anyone to know?

David: Well, my guess is that he doesn't want his parents to find out that he's been spending his time developing a better toilet paper holder when he should be studying for his final exams.

2 Listening for Information That is Divulged page 138

See Part 2 Listening for Signal Words on page 203 of this audioscript.

① Note-Taking Practice page 140

Student: Excuse me, Professor. I'm not sure that I really followed what you were saying yesterday in class about specific training in the arts not being an absolute necessity for creativity in the arts to emerge. Would you mind going over that again, please?

Professor: Sure. Let me illustrate my point about creativity this way. The neo-expressionist painter, Jean-Michel Basquiat began as a street graffiti artist in New York. Basquiat never had an art lesson in his life and yet his works are displayed in museums all over the world.

Student: Well, that's true, but he hung out with other artists and maybe some teachers. Couldn't he have picked up his skills from a teacher somewhere along the line?

Professor: He could have, but apparently he didn't. Furthermore, Basquiat is also an example of something else I said during our last class. This was about the equity of creativity. Let me repeat—and I really can't emphasize this enough—creativity is not linked to sex or age or race. It is not linked to any particular type of human being.

Student: Sure. I'm beginning to get what you were talking about. But didn't you also define creativity as being bound by time, place, and culture?

Professor: Well, sort of. What I was describing was that creativity can be crushed by a particular context or cultural environment that does not appreciate the creative efforts made by an individual in that place or at that time.

Student: Oh, I see. Basquiat is certainly an example of this. I'm sure that most people, older folks for sure, didn't appreciate his graffiti art all over their buildings, at first anyway. Would van Gogh be another good example of an artist whose work was not appreciated by the general public? You know, he couldn't seem to sell many of his paintings while he was alive, but now they're worth tens of millions of dollars.

Professor: Right on both counts. But the *reality* is that they *were creative* even though they were not appreciated. And later in Basquiat's career or after van Gogh died, their work did not *become* creative. Instead, it was the creative imaginations of the viewers of the art that had to catch up to, or rise to, the level of their creative visions. And sadly, that took a long time in van Gogh's case.

Student: Thanks so much for clarifying what you were getting at yesterday. That helped a lot. I just have one more question.

Professor: Yes, of course. Shoot.

Student: Well, this may sound a little naïve, but isn't everything, I mean absolutely everything we do, creative on some level? I mean can you give me examples of human activity that isn't creative?

Professor: Good for you! That's a challenging question! You've stimulated me to think further about this over the weekend, and I'll make time for you to lead a discussion on that topic on Monday, OK?

Question 1: What was the student confused about? (Choose two.)

Question 2: Why does the professor use Jean-Michel Basquiat as an illustration?

3. *Listen to part of the conversation again.*

Professor: Furthermore, Basquiat is also an example of something else I said during our last class. This was about the equity of creativity. Let me repeat—and I really can't emphasize this enough—creativity is not linked to sex or age or race.

Question 3: Why does the professor say "and I really can't emphasize this enough"?

Question 4: What does the professor imply about van Gogh's work? (Choose two.)

5. *Listen to part of the conversation again.*

Student: Well, this may sound a little naïve, but isn't everything, I mean absolutely everything we do, creative on some level? I mean, can you give me examples of human activity that isn't creative?

Question 5: Why does the student say, "This may sound a little naïve, but… "?

Lecture: Group Dynamics

Professor: This afternoon I'm going to talk about a topic that affects every person in this room—group dynamics. Every person in this room is part of some group, right? For example, you belong to this class. And I'm sure that you belong to other groups, too, don't you? Your family, right? A social club perhaps? A soccer, golf, or tennis team? The international student association? What else? Help me out.

Student A: Pi Phi sorority.

Student B: Exam study groups.

Student C: A business students' discussion group.

Student D: Volunteers for a Clean Environment.

Student E: Film Club.

Professor: Good. Thanks. At any one time the average person belongs to five or six different groups. A large part of our sense of identity comes from belonging to these groups. In fact, if I asked you to describe yourself, you might say, for example, "I'm a student, a basketball player, and a member of the film club," wouldn't you? Well today we're going to look at two interesting aspects of group dynamics, or how groups function. First, we'll look at patterns of communication in groups, and then we'll look at how groups affect individual performance.

In groups, communication seems unsystematic, random, and unplanned, doesn't it? Generally, we don't see any pattern of communication at all. By the way, you all went to the discussion section yesterday, didn't you? Well, what did you notice about the conversations?

Student B: Everyone kept interrupting me.

Professor: Yes! And if you were having a good discussion, people kept interrupting each other and talking at the same time, didn't they? I'll bet students talked pretty much whenever they wanted. Well, let's see what researchers have found concerning communication patterns and group dynamics or how groups function.

The first pattern they have found occurs in groups where there is a lively discussion. It seems like everyone is talking at once, but actually, only a few people are talking. And it doesn't seem to matter how large the group is—only a few people talk at once. Do you know how many? What do you think?

Student C: Three? A few is three, right?

Students: Three? Four? Two?

Professor: Yes, well, the answer is two. Two people do over fifty percent of the talking in any group.

Now let's look at the second pattern researchers found in group dynamics. When we're in a group, sitting around a table perhaps, who do we talk to? As an aside, I must tell you that all the research I know about has been done in the United States and Canada, so the results I have to share with you may only be valid for these countries. Well, as I started to say, who do people talk to when they're sitting together at a table—people across the table, or people sitting next to them?

Students: Across the table.
       Next to them.
       No, across.
       No, I'm sure it's next to them.

Professor: Well, the research shows that in groups of eight or more, people talk to the people sitting across the table from them, not to the people next to them. Why do we talk more to the people sitting opposite us? Probably because in our culture we usually make eye contact with the person we're talking to, and it's not as easy to have eye contact with someone who is sitting next to us. It's much easier to maintain eye contact with someone across the table.

To go somewhat off the topic for a moment, if you're planning to be a matchmaker and start a romance between two of your friends, don't seat them next to each other at your next dinner party. On second thought, maybe seating them at a corner of the table would be best, wouldn't it? Then they would be very near each other and would only have to turn slightly in order to look into each other's eyes.

Well, back to business. Now there's one more point that I'd like to mention regarding conversations in groups (and this might be important to the new romance at your dinner party. Who knows?). The research also shows that, in general, the person in the group who talks the most is regarded as the leader of the group. However, it's true that this person is not usually the most liked in the group, isn't it? D. J. Stang did some research that showed that the person in the group who talked only a moderate amount was liked the most. What use can we make of this information? A new romance would be affected by this aspect of group dynamics, wouldn't it?

But enough of romance and dinner parties. I now want to discuss another important aspect of group dynamics—the effect a group has on an individual's performance. The research tells us that sometimes the effect of the group on someone's performance is positive, and sometimes it's negative. It took quite a while for social psychologists to figure out why this is true.

Some research showed that people did better on a task when they were doing it in a group. It didn't matter what the task was, whether it was slicing tomatoes or racing bicycles; people just performed better when other people were there. It also didn't matter whether the other people in the group were doing the same task or just watching, so competition was not a factor. The first person to notice this phenomenon was Triplett.

Student A: Excuse me, but what was his first name? It wasn't Tom, was it?

Professor: I'm sorry, I don't remember. Please come by my office if you want the complete reference. Anyway, as I was saying, Triplett's research was done quite a long time ago. In 1898, in fact. He watched bicycle racers and noticed that they did much better when they raced against each other than when they raced only against the clock.

This behavior surprised him, so he conducted a simple experiment. He gave a group of children some fishing poles and string. The children were told to wind the string around the fishing poles as fast as possible. Half of the children worked alone. The others worked in pairs. Interestingly, the children who worked in pairs worked faster than those who worked alone.

Well, you're probably not interested in winding string around fishing poles faster, but you *are* interested in doing math problems better, aren't you? F. H. Allport had people work on math problems alone and also in groups of five to six. He found that people did better in the group situation than when they worked alone. The theory behind this type of research—research which demonstrates that people do better when they work in groups—is called social facilitation theory.

Let me digress a bit on this matter of having an audience. In this way, we're like a number of other creatures—ants, for example. Chen did a laboratory experiment with some ants as they were building nests. Chen had some of the ants work alone and some of the ants work with one or two other ants. Guess what! Ants worked harder when they worked with other ants than when they worked alone.

Another famous study was done with cockroaches. Zajonc, Heingartner, and Herman watched cockroaches find their way through a maze while trying to get away from a light. As you may know, cockroaches hate light. They are photophobic, right? The researchers had the cockroaches go through the maze with an audience of four other cockroaches. The cockroaches reached the end of the maze faster when they had an audience.

Students: No way!
Really?
You're kidding, right?

Professor: No, no! Really! This is true.

Well, to continue, as I mentioned earlier, there is also research that demonstrates the opposite—that individuals perform worse, not better, on tasks when other people are there! The theory behind this research, which shows that people do poorly in groups, is called social inhibition theory. R. W. Hubbard did an interesting experiment on this. He had people learn a finger maze. This is a maze that you trace with your finger. The people who had an audience did worse than the people who did the maze alone.

So, how can we explain these contradictory results? Zajonc finally came up with a possible reason why people sometimes perform better and sometimes worse in front of an audience. He found that the presence of an audience facilitates or helps you with what you already know how to do. That is, if you *know* what you are doing, having an audience helps you do it better. But if you *don't* already know how to do something, you will probably make some mistakes. And if you have an audience, you will continue to make mistakes. He pointed out that when you are first learning something, you are better off working alone than practicing with other people.

So to recap, the research shows that people generally perform better in groups, *except* if they are performing a new task. In that case they work better alone. And just let me mention in passing that if you can manage it, you should take tests on a stage in front of a large audience with a group of people who are also taking the test. Not very practical though, is it? And I wonder if it's really true for every task we learn. What do you think? Well, let's start with that question next time. See you then.

PART 3 Using Tag Questions to Ask for Information or Confirmation, or to Challenge

2 Listening for Intonation Patterns page 156

Conversation 1

Steven: Our team is having the first practice of the season this Saturday morning at 8:00. You'll be there, Tom, won't you?

Tom: Oh sure, I'll be there early.

Conversation 2

Steven: Our team is having the first practice of the season this Saturday morning at 8:00. You'll be there, George, won't you?

George: Sure will.

Conversation 3

Steven: Soccer practice is at 6:30 this Saturday morning because another team has the field at 8:30.

Tom: Steve, Karl told me he couldn't come to soccer practice until eight.

Steven: What a drag. He's always late. He thinks he's coming at eight, does he? Well, I think he's off the team, then. He can't come and go as he pleases and still be on the team.

Conversation 4

Boss: Charlie, I've got an unexpected merchandising meeting this week. The report won't be done by Wednesday, will it?

Charlie: Well, I don't think so, but we'll work on it.

Conversation 5

Josie: Hi, Pete. How are you?

Pete: Fine, how 'bout you?

Josie: Good. You're not cooking tonight, huh?

Pete: You got it. It's Bill's turn, right?

Josie: I think so, but he's going to be late again. I know it.

Pete: In that case, let's start the soup, OK? Otherwise, it'll be nine o'clock before we ever get anything to eat.

Josie: OK, you're right. I'm starving. You cut the carrots and I'll do the potatoes.

3 Listening for the Three Types of Tag Questions page 157

See Part 2 Recognizing Digressions on page 208 of this audioscript.

PART 4 Focus on Testing

1 Transition Phrases: Lecture page 161

Professor: Today we're going to look at something very familiar to you all—group work. You know, what teachers tell you to do when the teacher wants to relax. No, just kidding. Seriously, though, how many of you have done any group work in a class within, say, the last week? Wow. Almost everyone. Why do your teachers organize group work so much in their classes?

Student 1: Because it's easy.

Professor: Easy for whom? The teacher? The students?

Student 1: Everyone.

Professor: Well, I can speak from the teacher's perspective here. Group work is not especially easy to organize. By the way, we don't do much of it here because there are about 100 of us and this room is like a theater. If I had a better room... Well, never mind. I can assure you that group work, serious group work, requires a lot more planning on the teacher's part than lecturing does. Nothing could be easier than standing up here talking about anything I like. Now, from the student's point of view, is group work easy?

Student 2: Well... yes and no.

Professor: Could you give us some details? Why yes and why no?

Student 2: Well, it's easy because you don't have to do everything yourself. The group is responsible, not just you. But then again, the group can be a pain if they're not very good.

Professor: Beautiful. You've really brought up some important aspects of research on group work. Before we look at these, let me tell you where I stand on group work. I think it's great. All sorts of instructional advantages. But let me get to that later, if we have time. As you said, group work can take pressure off the individual, but it can also cause problems. Let's look at each of these points.

1. *Listen again to part of the lecture.*

Professor: You know, what teachers tell you to do when the teacher wants to relax. No, just kidding. Seriously, though, how many of you have done any group work in a class within, say, the last week.

Question 1: What does the professor mean when he says, "just kidding"?

Question 2: Why does the professor say "seriously"?

3. *Listen again to part of the lecture.*

Professor: By the way, we don't do much of it here because there are about 100 of us and this room is like a theater. If I had a better room... Well, never mind.

Question 3: Why does the professor say, "by the way"?

Question 4: What does the professor mean when he says, "Well, never mind"?

5. *Listen again to part of the lecture.*

Professor: Before we look at these, let me tell you where I stand on group work. I think it's great. All sorts of instructional advantages. But let me get to that later, if we have time.

Question 5: What does the professor indicate by saying, "But let me get to that later"?

CHAPTER 10

Crime and Punishment

PART 2 Paraphrasing

③ Listening to Paraphrase Parts of a Lecture page 170

Lecture: Human Choice—Predetermination or Free Will?

Professor: OK, let's get started. Today's lecture about choice is in two parts. The first part of the lecture is about the difference between predetermination and free will. I hope that by the end of class that difference will be clear to you all, because I want to hear your ideas on these two very different views of the world. The second part of the lecture is about choice in the real world—when life-or-death decisions have to be made.

So, do you believe that our lives are predetermined, or do you believe that we make choices that direct our lives? Basically, if you believe that our lives are predetermined, then you believe that everything we do is decided before we are born. Maybe you think we are programmed to do the things we do. Or perhaps you think a spiritual force makes all our decisions for us. But even if we believe our lives are somehow predetermined, we still appear to be making choices every day. We choose what to have for dinner or what movie to go to. We choose our friends from among the hundreds of people we meet. So the question is: Are these really choices, or is the concept of free choice only an illusion?

On the other hand, if you believe that we have free will, then you believe that we do really make all our own decisions. For example, Hindus and Buddhists believe that our choices are made freely and that these choices add up to either a good life or a bad life. This is called *karma*. They also believe in reincarnation. According to this belief, if we don't make enough good decisions during one lifetime, we are reborn to try to do better in the next life.

These two opposing views, predetermination and free will, can have important effects on our lives. How do you think they can affect us? Yes, Craig?

Student 1: Well, if you believe that everything is predetermined… then that might make you feel as if you have no control over what happens to you… you know… no control over your life.

Student 2: And that feeling would certainly affect your behavior. For example, maybe you would feel that if you are not in control, then you don't have to take responsibility for your choices.

Professor: Yes, that's quite possible. Therefore, we should examine these opposing views about choice as a starting point in determining our own attitude toward life. You may recall that Socrates suggested this when he said that the "unexamined life is no worth living."

How many of you have looked at your past actions and said, "I wish I had done that differently" or "If only I had decided to do this instead of what I did"? And certainly, we all have worried about the future and thought, "I hope I can do the right thing." Our relationship to the past and to the future seems to be connected with our present choices. That is, all our wishes and hopes for the future are very connected to what we choose now, in the present.

Stop 1

Professor: Now let's talk about choice in the real world. The practical implications of choice increase and intensify when life-or-death decisions have to be made. For example, if you were a judge and your job was to sentence a person to prison or even death for violation of rules or beliefs in your community, you might question the nature of right and wrong before finally reaching a decision. Do any of you recall the character Jean Valjean from *Les Miserables*, who was sentenced to seven years of slavery for stealing a loaf of bread for his starving family? What choice would you have made if you were the judge? I hope you are compassionate and would take time to consider all the possible choices and not decide too quickly.

Students: Wow. That's a tough one. I don't know. I'm really not sure. I need to think about it.

Professor: And what if you were Jean Valjean? Would you have chosen to break the law to feed your family?

Students: Absolutely! Of course! I'd have to! You bet your life I would!

Stop 2

Professor: OK. All right then. But now I want you to think about this. Would you then say that you were not really responsible for the crime? Would you try to get off, be excused, by saying you did it because the society did not provide a job for you and that's why you and your family were so hungry? This is not an easy question, is it?

Now, what about this case? On March 30th, 1981, the president of the United States, Ronald Reagan, and three other men were shot on a street in Washington, DC. John Hinckley, Jr., the young man who shot these men, admitted that he felt no remorse about his crime. Three of his four victims recovered; the fourth suffered permanent brain damage.

Fifteen months later, after an eight-week trial that cost three million dollars, Hinckley was found "not guilty by reason of insanity." Think about that. Hinckley shot the president of the United States and three other people and was only sent to a mental hospital for counseling and treatment. When the psychiatrists decide that he is well enough, he will be released and sent home. He will not go to prison.

Student 1: Wow! That's incredible!

Student 2: That's terrible!

Student 3: No kidding! I didn't know that!

Professor: Well, it's true. Naturally, many people were very angry that Hinckley received such a small punishment. However, Hinckley's punishment is not my focus here. I want to focus instead on the choice Hinckley made. His actions came from his choice, and his actions injured four people.

Did you know that in the United States, only those criminals who made their choices consciously, willfully, and freely are punished? Yup, that's the law. If it is proven in court that an act, no matter how evil, was caused by influences beyond the control of the person who did it, then that person is not punished for the act.

In other words, in American society, the law says that you are not responsible for choices you make if you are not aware or in control of your actions. This is called legal insanity. How about that!?

Stop 3

Professor: We are faced with other questions—perhaps not as serious—every moment of our lives. Who will I go out with on Saturday night? Shall I go on a diet? Should I go to the movies tonight or should I study for that biology test? Should I make long-range plans for my career? And more important, how should I treat other people?

The poetry, fiction, and theater of every culture reflect the drama involved in making these kinds of choices, but they do not offer simple answers. The only definite rule we are given about making choices is that we have to make them or they will be made for us. Ah, but if only we could make perfect choices, then there would be no problem, right?

In summary, we have touched lightly on the extremely important matter of the nature of human choice and briefly examined the relationship between human choice, crime, and punishment. I hope this lecture has stimulated you to reflect on your own choices—what they are and why you are making them—and to consider how they shape your worldview and what your responsibility is for their effects. And remember: Whether you think your choices are predetermined or made freely, you cannot get away from making choices, for after all, to choose is to be human.

PART 3 Wishes, Hopes, and Desires

1 Listening for Wishes, Hopes, and Desires page 173

Laura: Have you found a house to rent yet?

James: No, not yet. I hope I find one soon. My family is arriving in a few days, and I want to have a house ready for them when they get here.

Laura: Sounds like you could use some help.

James: Well, maybe a little, but probably all I really need is more money. If only I didn't have

to find something inexpensive. I wish I were making more money. Then I would have more choices of houses.

Laura: Well, I may be able to help you out there.

James: You mean you know of a good house for us?

Laura: Not exactly. But I might know of a way for you to make some easy money making some quick deliveries.

James: Uh-oh. This sounds too easy to be legal. But I tell you, I'm getting really desperate at this point. I just might be tempted anyway.

Laura: Well, I certainly hope you're kidding. But you don't have to worry. It's definitely legal. I heard that Pizza Time wants someone to deliver pizzas from 6:00 to 9:00 every night. And the pay's not bad.

James: Oh, is that all? Well, that sounds great! Who do I talk to?

2 Listening to Paraphrase Wishes, Hopes, and Desires page 174

See Part 2 Paraphrasing on page 211 of this audioscript.

PART 4 Focus on Testing

1 Idea-Connection Questions: Lecture page 177

Professor: I think you're all familiar with the age-old debate over free will and predetermination. But recent medical research has added an entirely new dimension to it. In the past, it was mostly a question of whether (1) humans are free to make their own choices or (2) those choices are made for us by some higher power. Now, there's a third choice: My chemicals made me do it.

Neuroscience has identified about thirty-five chemicals—the neurotransmitters—that help carry messages throughout the brain. Let's use one of them, serotonin, as an example.

One of the first clues pointing to some relation between serotonin and crime came from a large Dutch family whose males were known for particularly violent behavior. Researchers who analyzed the brain chemistry of some family members found a chemical problem. The men had very low levels of MAOA, a chemical that breaks down serotonin. This suggested that too much serotonin could lead to violent behavior.

Later experiments indicated that too *little* serotonin might have the same effect. Violent and impulsive individuals were found to have brain cells that soaked up serotonin very fast. Since this neurotransmitter was known to calm certain people down, researchers reasoned that increasing serotonin levels would solve the problem. Drugs called SSRIs were developed to slow down the re-uptake, or absorbing, of serotonin. They seemed to work. In fact, I think you've all heard of one SSRI, Prozac. It was so effective that it became one of the largest-selling medications of all time.

Anyway, the bottom line is that no one knows exactly how serotonin—or any of its thirty-some chemical cousins—really works. It has some relation to criminal violence, but what? Is too much worse than too little? I suspect the answer will involve a lot of factors, a lot of interactions among chemicals, environmental conditions, and even personal experiences. But I'm just guessing.

The one thing we know for sure is that scientific research into brain chemistry is already influencing the criminal courts. If you commit a violent crime because your brain chemicals are out of balance, are you really responsible? Judges have long ruled that a "legally insane" person, a person who cannot distinguish between "right" and "wrong," is not necessarily responsible for his or her crimes. Neuroscience might simply be discovering the chemical reasons for this insanity.

The principle is being tested in the Nevada courts in the case of a young man whom I'll call Jason. Jason was arrested in a hotel lobby, and he quickly admitted that he had, in fact, just committed a murder. A hotel video camera showed him at the scene of the crime. His defense lawyers do not dispute that, unfortunately, he killed someone. However, they have argued that Jason's genetic background is to blame. Jason was raised by a loving and nonviolent adoptive father and mother, but investigators found that his biological parents and two brothers lived disturbingly violent lives. All had histories of violently aggressive behavior, mental illness, or both. Jason himself had been diagnosed with serious attention deficit disorder, ADD. The disorder is very often found in people whose brains lack enough serotonin. Further tests of Jason's brain chemistry will reveal more about this troubled young man, but some genetically-based chemical problem is likely. His family's history of criminal behavior goes back more than one hundred years.

Jason was eighteen years old when he committed murder, so he was legally an adult. But is he legally responsible for the crime? Those who say *no* point out that he has no control over the chemistry of his brain. Under the influence of that chemistry, they say, he could not make a free choice about what he should do. They also point out that he was seeking medical help for his problems, which indicates a desire to get better. Those who do hold him responsible say that body chemistry can affect decisions but does not make them. After all, the definition of legal insanity is very narrow: Not comprehending the difference between "right" and "wrong." And Jason, in seeking help, showed that he did understand that difference. Almost everyone has unfortunate influences in life. We have a social obligation, they say, to overcome those limitations, to choose wisely anyway.

Question 1: According to the professor, what was one of the first indications of a connection between serotonin levels and violent behavior?

Question 2: In the lecture, the professor mentions some support for the belief that people freely choose whether to commit a crime or not. She also mentions arguments for the opposite—a lack of free choice. Indicate which position each statement supports. Mark an "X" in the proper box for each statement.

Question 3: According to the professor, why is it sometimes helpful to reduce the speed at which serotonin is absorbed by brain cells?

Question 4: Why does the professor start the lecture by mentioning free will and predetermination?

Chapter 1 | Part 3

Talk It Over pages 19–20

1. Zero, because 0 times *anything* is 0.

2. Turn on the first two switches and leave them on for 5 minutes. After 5 minutes, turn off the second switch, leaving the first switch on. Now go upstairs to the attic. The light that is on is connected to the first switch. The light that is off, but has a bulb that is still warm to the touch, is connected to the second switch. The light that is both off and cold to the touch is connected to the third switch, which was never turned on.

3. The word *wheat* becomes *heat* if you remove the first letter, *eat* if you remove the first two letters, and *tea* if you scramble the last three letters.

4. Fill the 5 gallon jug with water; pour it into the 3 gallon jug until the 3 gallon is full, leaving 2 gallons in the 5 gallon jug. Now pour out the water in the 3 gallon jug. Pour the 2 gallons of water (in the 5 gallon jug) into the empty 3 gallon jug. Fill the 5 gallon jug. You now have exactly 7 gallons!

5. NONE! Roosters don't lay eggs!

6. The man waited for nightfall. Once it was dark, he exited through the door to the room made of magnifying glass.

7. There is no extra dollar. You and your friend paid $30 total for the bill—$25 of it went for the food, $3 went for the tip, and each of you got a dollar back, for a grand total of $30.

Chapter 6 | Part 1

Vocabulary Preview page 94

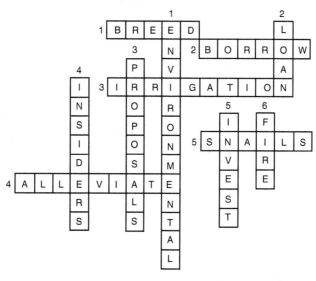

Vocabulary Index

Skills Index